CONTENTS

INTRODUCTION 4

CHAPTER 1: HOME DÉCOR 7
Candle Luminaries 9
Phone Book Letter Holder 12
Crepe Paper Lilacs 16
Tiered Garland Ornament 22
Citrus Slice Coasters 24
Sticky Notes Notepad Holder 28
Mysterious Stationery Box 32
Silhouette Portrait Art 41

CHAPTER 2: FASHION ACCESSORIES 45
Tiger Lily Fascinator 46
Everyday Tote Bag 51

CHAPTER 3: JEWELRY 55
Jungle Beads Necklace 56
Introduction to Quilling 58
Teardrop Orb Pendant 59
Antique Key Pendant 65
Fine Paper Yarn Necklace 68
Loosely Braided Makigami Pendant 72
Makigami Pendant Flower 78

CHAPTER 4: CORRESPONDENCE 83
Frameable Tree Card 84
Perfect Journey Journal 88
Frameable Gift Card 94
Wedding Cake Card 100
Fringed Flower Card 104

ARTIST GALLERY AND DIRECTORY 106
TEMPLATES 108

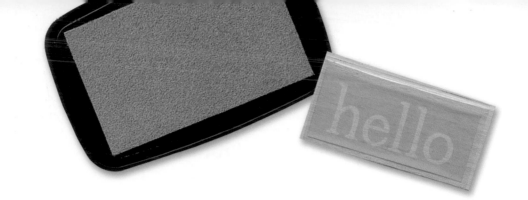

DISCOVER A NEW HOBBY

When I began blogging, the goal was to share my love of the many creative things that can be done with paper, and to also introduce those who work with this humble medium to the world. I wasn't positive there would be an audience, but surprise, surprise, there certainly was! One of the very best perks of blogging has been the people I've met around the world and featured on my website, as they are all such inspiring souls. Of course, tutorials are always extremely popular because those of us who enjoy reading about the latest ideas in the world of paper crafting are also usually interested in trying our hand at actually making them.

But as often as I turn to the Internet for inspiration, there's nothing quite like feeling the smooth pages of a book in my hands and leaving one open on my work table as a quick and easy reference. So what better thing to do than ask some of my favorite paper artisans to create a bevy of brand new projects complete with step-by-step instructions? You can imagine my excitement at gathering a delightful collection between two covers!

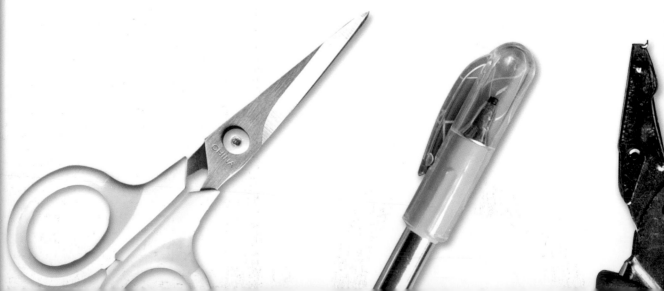

Here you'll find home décor ideas, fashion and jewelry accessories, along with greeting cards and a journal, all from eighteen designers—a true expression of hands-across-papercrafts. I hope the projects will cause you to look at paper in a new light. Many are eco-friendly, and all are stylish and functional. Create a garden of pretty flowers with crépe, fringed, mulberry, and metallic papers. Be surprised by eye-catching accessories that are sure to attract the most sophisticated wearer, and make necklaces from rolled, folded, or punched paper. Learn novel techniques for fabricating rope from an unexpected material, stitching on paper, and even crocheting with paper! Discover wall décor that ranges from ever-popular hand cut silhouettes to the use of paper scraps as a dual-purpose art gift.

Paging through the book will uncover a variety of new concepts—some are quite simple and others are more involved. Beginners will be able to replicate many of the projects, the majority of which use readily available supplies. Gain new skills such as screen printing, bookbinding, paper cutting, and box making. You'll find complete instructions, diagrams, and templates. So dig in, lose track of time, and most of all, have fun. No doubt you'll quickly determine the areas of paper crafting that draw you in, bringing joy and satisfaction. Here's to finding a new hobby that may last a lifetime!

Ann Martin

Ann Martin

author of *All Things Paper*

allthingspaper.net

The projects in this book are dimensioned with Imperial/English units (inches) with Metric units following (cm/mm). The metric conversions are rounded for convenience, so please ensure care when measuring to the published numbers. Often these dimensions should be interpreted as mere suggestions and you, the artist, are encouraged to follow the projects according to your own supplies, tools, and vision.

CHAPTER 1
HOME DÉCOR

Eye-catching projects to beautify
your desk, dining table, and walls.

CANDLE LUMINARIES

by Kristen Magee

These pretty paper luminaries are a very easy and inexpensive way to add a little pizzazz to your table for a special occasion or just because. Make a few to complement other decorative accessories, or make many and group them together to create a glowing tablescape.

SUPPLIES AND TOOLS

Small glass or cylinder vase
Copy paper white
Pencil
Measuring tape
Ruler
Scissors
Decorative edge scissors (scalloped and clouds)
  and/or pinking shears
Hole punches a variety of sizes
Tape runner or double-sided tape
Tealight candle or battery operated tealight
Paper trimmer optional

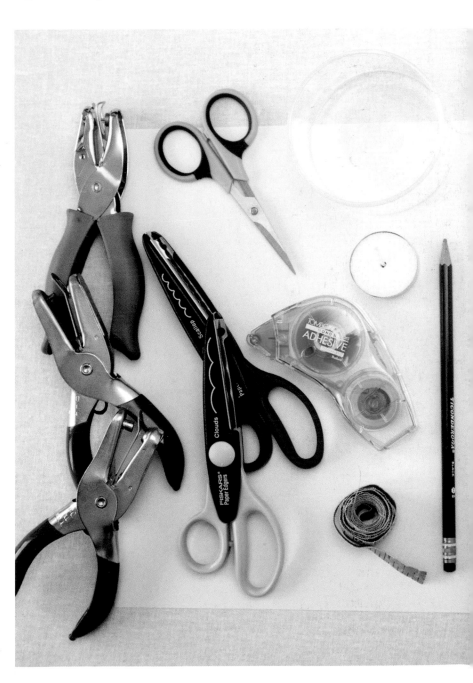

Kristen Magee

A freelance designer who loves to craft and cook in her spare time, Kristen shares her love of paper as the editor of *Paper Crave* **papercrave.com** and documents her craft and kitchen exploits at *Domestifluff* **domestifluff.com**

Why Paper?

I love working with paper because it's such a versatile and accessible medium. There's nothing more relaxing to me after a long day in front of the computer than sitting down with a few sheets of paper to fold, score, and cut to my heart's content.

HOW TO MAKE THE CANDLE LUMINARIES

STEP 1 Measure the circumference and height of the container with a measuring tape. Add approximately ½ inch (13 mm) to the circumference so there will be enough paper to overlap when it is wrapped around the container.

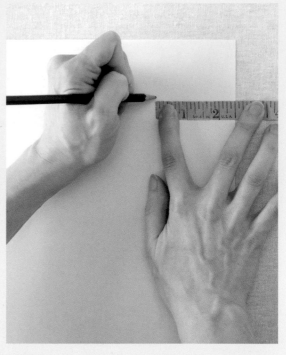

STEP 2 Use a pencil to mark the length and width on a piece of copy paper. Draw corresponding lines with the aid of a ruler. Use scissors or a paper trimmer to cut the paper.

STEP 3 Cut along one edge of the paper with decorative edge scissors or pinking shears. Be sure to stay as close to the edge as possible, using it as a cutting guide.

STEP 4 Pierce a hole with a small hole punch in the center of each scallop or pinked V. It may be helpful to dot the centers with a pencil before using the punch. This allows for more precise placement.

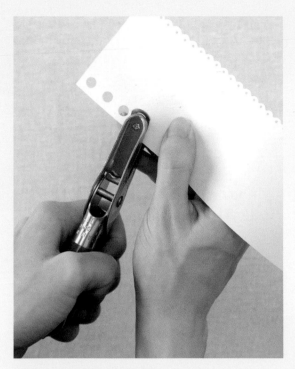

STEP 5 Use a larger punch to make a row of evenly spaced holes along the bottom edge of the paper.

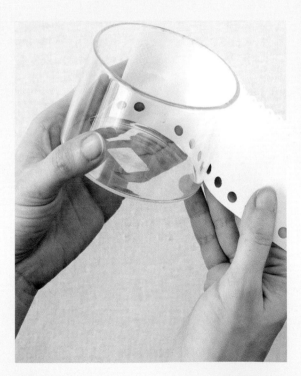

STEP 6 Apply a strip of double-sided tape to one end of the paper. Wrap the paper snugly around the container, overlapping the ends. Try different papers—vellum, parchment, or tissue—for a variety of looks.

PHONE BOOK LETTER HOLDER

by Allison Patrick

At least once a year a stack of phone books arrives in my building lobby where they languish for a few weeks until someone bundles them up for the recycling pile. In this Internet age you might not need old fashioned phone books for looking up information, but they can be put to good use and help with organization at the same time, as this pretty mail sorter demonstrates. It's the perfect accessory for a front hallway or desk. Not only is it eco-friendly to use an otherwise discarded material, but the project cost is low because the phone book is free. The petal design looks elegant even when not in use, and I love the bright pop of colorful ribbons that can be chosen to match the color scheme of any room. This project is not only fun and recycles wasted paper but is also functional and decorative. The finished letter holder measures 7 x 4 inches (18 x 10 cm). Because the phone book is divided in half and then cut into strip sections, quite a few letter holders can be made from just one phone book!

Allison Patrick

A recent graduate with a Master of Architecture degree from Columbia University, Allison Patrick began designing eco-friendly housewares and lights in 2010. Selling both in person and via Etsy shops, Zipper 8 Design and Zipper 8 Lighting, allows her to fund all those crazy and creative projects she wants to try, while following a more eclectic path professionally. Her recent work experience includes an internship in the exhibition design department at The Solomon R. Guggenheim Museum and teaching lower school science in New York City. Looking for a place to showcase the more random craft projects she undertakes, Allison started her blog, The 3 Rs: Reduce, Reuse, Redecorate. She features projects for the home that are based on unusual and eco-friendly materials, often bringing new life to otherwise overlooked items. Her work has been featured on numerous blogs and in magazines, as well as on the cover of *Illuminate*, Hannah Nunn's 2012 contemporary craft lighting book.

Website: zipper8lighting.com
Blog: the3rsblog.wordpress.com

Why Paper?

Paper is one of my favorite crafting materials. Whether bought new or reused from another source, paper is inexpensive and accessible. Even if I buy fine quality paper for an intended project, I can first practice on a much less expensive kind. Paper is also more versatile than almost any material. It can be a thin, flat sheet or with just a few creases, transformed into a complex, three-dimensional shape. Layer it to create texture or wrap it around something like a skin. And everyone has access to paper no matter where they are—grab a newspaper off the street or a sheet from a printer. The most amazing creations can be made with just a bit of imagination, allowing the mind of the artist to shine through."

SUPPLIES AND TOOLS

Phone book Choose one with a fairly small width and length because a larger phone book may cause the loops to be floppy. The one used here measured 6.75 x 8.5 inches (17 x 22 cm) and was 1.75 inches (5 cm) thick.

Colorful ribbon 1-2 inches (2.5-5 cm) wide by approximately 60 inches (152 cm) long

Corrugated cardboard

Cutting mat

Scissors

Scrap paper

Paper clips

Glue gun with glue sticks

Metal ruler A metal ruler is always better than a plastic or wooden one when working with a cutting blade because the metal can't be accidentally sliced.

Extendable cutting blade I use Olfa; X-ACTO makes them too.

HOW TO MAKE THE LETTER HOLDER

STEP 1 Open the phone book at its midpoint and cut through the center of the spine with a cutting blade or scissors to make equal halves. Working with one of the halves, cut a section of pages across the top or bottom that is the same width as the ribbon. Remove the remaining cover piece.

STEP 2 Cut a 3½-inch (9 cm) piece of corrugated cardboard that is the same width as the ribbon. Glue the phone book spine to the center of the cardboard piece.

STEP 3 Use scrap paper as bookmarks to subdivide the phone book segment into seven sections. The five center sections should be twice as thick as the two outer sections. Although the following may sound complicated at first, an easy way to do this is to divide the phone book into four equal sections and then subdivide each quarter into three sections, resulting in twelve equal sections. Then use a single subdivided piece for each of the outer two sections, but use two of the subdivided pieces for each of the center five sections. Once the sections are subdivided, keep them separate by paper clipping each one as a unit until it is time to roll it.

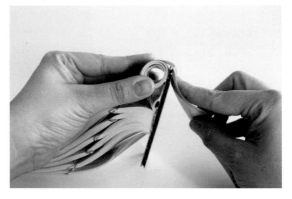

STEP 4 Pull six sections to the left, leaving one section to lean toward the right. Squeeze hot glue into the divide and insert the end of the ribbon. Take the single section (number 1) and roll it tightly outward until it reaches the cardboard. Holding the roll in place, squeeze glue onto the cardboard near the right edge, and carefully glue the ribbon so that it holds this section in its tight roll.

STEP 5 Turn the unit around and roll the other exterior section (number 7) into a tight, outward-facing roll to match the first section. Hold it in place while squeezing glue into the seam between the two sections (numbers 6 and 7) and press the ribbon in place, using a ruler to tuck it closely to the spine.

STEP 6 Take the next section (number 6) and subdivide it into three pieces. Curve the two pieces inward toward one another, using the third piece on the left to wrap over and around them.

Tips!

To make the cut through the depth of the phone book section, hold the ruler down very tightly and start slicing through the pages with a sharp, extendable cutting blade. Cut slowly over and over, trying not to slice through too much at once. Keep a firm grip on the ruler so it will hold the bulk of the book in place, resulting in an even cut. The slice doesn't have to be perfect, however, because once the letter holder has been rolled, the imperfections won't be noticeable.

The section that is being sliced off will slide away from the cut line so it is easier to see. Continue slicing and extending the blade until the book section is sliced completely through.

STEP 7 Once again squeeze glue into the seam between the two sections (numbers 5 and 6) and use the ruler to press the ribbon into place.

STEP 8 Repeat Steps 6 and 7 for the next section.

Tip!

In lieu of cutting your phone book with a craft blade, check with your local office supply store. It may have an industrial paper cutter that can slice through any book with ease.

STEP 9 Take the center section (number 4) and divide it into two pieces. Curve the left piece toward the center, then curve the right piece over and around the left piece, bringing the ribbon with it. Glue the ribbon into the seam between the two sections (numbers 3 and 4).

STEP 10 Repeat steps 6 and 7 for the final two sections.

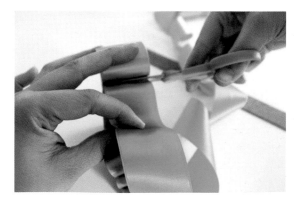

STEP 11 After the ribbon has been glued over the last of these sections, it will be back at the first tight roll that was glued in place, and where the ribbon began between sections 1 and 2. Cut off any remaining ribbon close to the binding.

Add mail or other papers that need sorting and enjoy!

CREPE PAPER LILACS
by Jenny Jafek-Jones

Spring comes to my studio in a riot of color; the faded browns and grays of winter disappear in a matter of days. A little rain and sunshine together make the clay of the red dirt road vibrant again, and emerald clumps of clover cause the colors to pop even more.

Many of my favorite people live in other states and big cities, so my local flora doesn't represent spring to them in quite the same manner. When I send them flowers to celebrate the season, I go with a classic: lilacs. They're gorgeous.

Many people associate lilacs with childhood memories and family time, but for me, lilacs also signify the renewing aspect of springtime. In the Victorian language of flowers, they represent youthful innocence and the first emotions of love.

I realize that the incredible fragrance of lilacs is part of their charm. The trade-off in making them from paper is a good one though: no sneezing and sniffling if you have allergies, no fighting off bees, and the flowers will bloom when watering is forgotten.

As the recipient, you're assured that someone thought enough of you to put everything aside for a couple of hours in order to make you something beautiful. As the maker, you put a little of yourself into a project that can literally bring someone joy for years to come. That's a reward of its own.

Tips!
Doublette brand crepe paper is sold in folds and typically features two shades of a color, one on each side. Each fold measures approximately 10 x 48 inches (25 x 122 cm). A single fold of each color (green and lavender) is more than adequate for the project.

Sunrise brand wrapped wire is sold in packs of 25 and measures 14 inches (36 cm) in length; wrapped wire at createforless.com is sold in packs of 20 and measures 18 inches (46 cm) in length. A single pack is adequate for the project, although two wouldn't be a bad idea.

SUPPLIES AND TOOLS

Doublette crepe paper pale/olive green and lavender/pink lilac (castleintheair.biz)

Floral wire #22 green wrapped (budget version - createforless.com; best quality - Sunrise floral wire via amazon.com)

Glue I swear by Crafter's Pick "The Ultimate!" and transfer it to a fine-tip glue bottle for controlled application. You may use your favorite brand of glue, but from someone who uses glue ten hours a day and counts on it to make a living, go with the Crafter's Pick.

Scissors I like Fiskars 5" Softouch Spring Action.

Wire cutters

Mini binder clips a dozen or so is adequate

Petal pattern (page 109) photocopy at least 9 patterns onto plain paper for easy snipping

Jenny Jafek-Jones

The gardener for *the crimson poppy* forgets to water her houseplants, and like her mother, was not born with a green thumb. To compensate, she spends hours tending and trimming ordinary paper until it blooms into delicate petals and leaves. The beauty and attention to detail that hallmark her exquisite paper flowers has been recognized in *BRIDES, Paper Runway,* and *Southern Wedding* magazines, as well as numerous wedding and paper-related websites. Paper flowers from *the crimson poppy* were featured in celebrity gift lounges and swag bags for the 2012 Golden Globes and Academy Awards nominees, presenters, and attendees.

Jenny resides in with her family and eighteen pair of scissors in Dallas, Texas. Her paper flowers enchant recipients around the globe.

Website: thecrimsonpoppy.com
Blog: thecrimsonpoppy.tumblr.com

" Why Paper?

The crimson poppy and I have come a long way in the last few years. When I remarried in May of 2009, I decided I'd tackle the flowers myself by using the Internet as a how-to guide. I came across *kusudama* flowers that bring a lovely, whimsical effect to a wedding, but I preferred more realistic paper flowers. During the next six months I broadened my knowledge through floral punch art and Martha Stewart paper flower kits, and took the advice of friends and family to start selling the cards and decorated items I'd created, thus *the crimson poppy*. The fire for perfectly realistic paper flowers that wouldn't droop or wilt was lit. While selling at local craft shows and our small-town crafters' mall, I searched for patterns, learned more about shaping paper, and took apart fresh flowers to create templates. I still like to play with whimsical flowers for cards and wedding favors, but my passion is handcrafting incredibly realistic paper flowers.

I love making a connection with my customers, whether we're finding the right flowers for an arrangement to gift or building a work-of-art bridal bouquet that fulfills dreams held since childhood. The current work-in-progress for *tcp* is "make your own extraordinary paper flower" kits, about which I'm very excited. It's wonderful to bring a little beauty into someone else's day! I'm excited to say that I no longer have to balance a "day job" with my passion for paper flowers; a reorganization at the office provided the opportunity to just do it, and I jumped in totally unprepared. I wanted the freedom to be creative and still attend my daughter's Friday morning school assemblies before the opportunity was gone. Making paper flowers is a dream come true. From *the crimson poppy* to you, best wishes. May you bloom and grow! "

HOW TO MAKE THE CREPE PAPER LILACS

STEP 1a Clip the scalloped strip pattern to the lavender/pink lilac crepe paper. Fold another layer of crepe paper beneath the first, removing and replacing mini binder clips one at a time to secure the pattern to both layers.

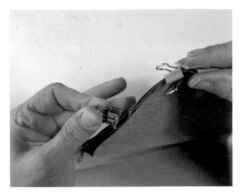

STEP 1b Repeat for a total of three layers, which will be cut simultaneously.

STEP 2 Cut a strip of folded crepe paper that is approximately ¼ inch (6 mm) wider than the pattern piece.

Tips!

Crepe paper has too much stretch to cut with scallop scissors, rotary cutters, and cutting machines. Regular scissors and a pattern are all that work.

Gathering the strip at step 4 makes it much easier to gather around the wire later. It's also a lot faster to gather the entire strip than each individual floret.

STEP 3a Cut out the pattern shape by snipping into the space between the petals from one direction, then come back up the row from the other end, leaving a pointed, triangular tip.

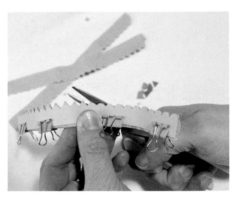

STEP 3b Round off the points; super-fast and easy!

STEP 4 Once the paper strips have been cut, remove the clips. Gently clasp one end of a strip between thumb and forefinger. Starting an inch (2.5 cm) or so from the clasped end, use the other hand to push the paper into a gathered fold. Repeat for the length of the strip, using the thumb and forefinger that are clasping the end to hold the gathered portion of the paper strip.

STEP 5 Lots of little flowers will be needed, so unfurl the strip and snip into it, making straight cuts halfway across the width between the first three rounded tops, then cut all the way through the paper strip after the fourth. Individual petals should look like those in the background of the photo. Repeat until there are at least 120 of the 4-round petals; I typically use 300 per lilac.

STEP 6 Use wire cutters to snip three pieces of wire, each approximately 2 inches (5 cm) in length, and a fourth measuring 3 inches (7.6 cm).

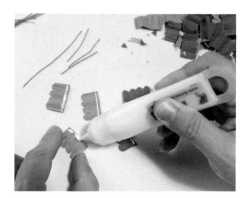

STEP 7a Squeeze a very thin bead of glue along the bottom of a petal; the amount needed as shown in the photo is exaggerated for easier viewing, so go easy!

STEP 7b Place one of the wire pieces in the glue at the far end of the petal. If you're left-handed, the end opposite the one shown in the photo might be more comfortable...whichever works best is fine.

STEP 7c Gather and pinch the base, wrapping the petal around the wire. Gathering is important to ensure the petal sections stay distinct and separate.

STEP 7d The final petal edge will overlap the first just a bit to secure it.

STEP 7e Use a fingernail or the edge of a closed pair of scissors to gently pull each petal piece outward. The motion should be similar to curling ribbon over a scissors blade. Repeat step 7 for the remaining three lengths of wire.

STEP 8 Use scissors to cut a narrow strip about 1/2 inch (13 mm) wide, across the grain of the folded green doublette crepe paper.

Tips!

Using both shades of the Doublette paper when making individual blooms will create subtle depth and additional color in the finished lilac.

If lilacs in a single color are preferred, be sure to put the glue on the same side (shade) of the Doublette paper for each individual bloom.

STEP 9 Apply a thin bead of glue to the green paper strip. Again, the amount of glue shown in the photo is exaggerated so it can be seen clearly; start with half as much for best results.

STEP 10a Gather four blooms together with the longest wire protruding from the bottom of the bunch. The tops should be somewhat level with one another, but not perfectly so.

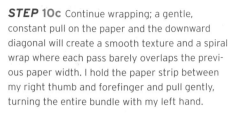

STEP 10c Continue wrapping; a gentle, constant pull on the paper and the downward diagonal will create a smooth texture and a spiral wrap where each pass barely overlaps the previous paper width. I hold the paper strip between my right thumb and forefinger and pull gently, turning the entire bundle with my left hand.

STEP 10d Wrap the green strip just past the end of the longest wire, cut it, and pinch the glued paper to complete the wrap. Congratulations! There is now one small bunch of lilac blooms. It takes practice, but after making three or four bunches, perfect ones will most likely be made in half the time. Make at least 26 finished bunches. The more that are made, the fuller the finished lilac will be. I typically use 75 bunches per lilac.

STEP 10b Place the end of the paper strip behind the wires, about halfway down the smaller lengths. Make one loop around the group of wires to secure them, and angle the green strip downward on a diagonal.

STEP 11 Use green paper and glue to wrap two of the wrapped 4-bloom bunches together. This wrap shouldn't be perfect or run the full length of the stems; just one or two passes around the middle of the bundles to secure them is fine. Repeat with the remaining bundles.

STEP 12a Make the central stem: wrap a length of 22 gauge wire in green paper in the same manner as the small lilac bundles. Starting about an inch (2.5 cm) from one end, wrap the entire length. When the far end is reached, continue just past the tip of the wire.

STEP 12b While the green paper strip is extended, add an extra dab of glue and fold the paper back onto the wire in a straight line. This will create a fold in the green strip similar to that of a flat sheet at the foot of a bed or gift wrap at the corner of a square package.

STEP 12c Place a thumb over this area to secure it and return to spiral wrapping. Be sure the first circle of wrap covers part of the fold, binding it to the earlier layer of stem wrap.

STEP 12d Continue wrapping the length of wire and cover the other end. When finished, there should be two layers of stem wrap and covered ends on the wire.

STEP 12e Fold the wrapped length of wire in half and pinch it so the two halves rest flat against one another. (The photo shows the loop for illustrative purposes only.) Use a strip of green paper and the spiral wrapping technique to secure the halves to one another, creating a sturdy central stem for the lilac.

STEP 13a More stem wrap; you're going to be an expert at this! Use a 1/2-inch (13 mm) green paper strip to attach one of the combined lilac bundles securely to the top of the central stem.

STEP 13b Attach another bundle of lilacs to the stem with the green strip; this one should go on the left side of the central stem and below the first.

STEP 13c Repeat on the right side, creating a triangular shape.

STEP 13d Turn the stem 90 degrees to the right and add a lilac bundle to the empty spaces on the left and right.

STEP 13e Repeat with the remaining lilac bundles, adding them to the central stem just below the previous level. The goal is to add lilac bundles in a fashion that covers the central stem and all of the wrappings, creating a gently rounded cone of blooms.

STEP 14 Optional: I cut a few leaf shapes from the green paper, glued a 3 inch (7.6 cm) piece of wire to the bottom 1/2-inch (13 mm) of the leaf, then pinched and held the leaf around the wire for a moment while the glue set to hide it within. The leaves were added to the base of the lilac to help cover the final stem wrappings and lilac bundles. Feel free to add a few leaves to the bloom while wrapping the central stem, leaving about 1/2 inch (13 mm) of each leaf stem outside the wrap. This allows the leaf to be bent down and out from the lilacs.

STEP 15a The stem wrap will be a bit bulky at the points where the lilac bundles were attached. Use the scissors point to make tiny snips into the green wrap at these places.

STEP 15b Use the fine-tip glue bottle to add the smallest drop of glue possible to the snipped area. I've exaggerated the glue for illustrative purposes again; the amount of glue in the photo is four or five times more than should be used.

STEP 15c Use a fingernail or toothpick to press the paper ends into the glue.

All done! Depending on how many bundles of blooms were made, the flower may look like this "just beginning to bloom" lavender lilac stem, or like the very full white lilacs on the right in a custom wedding bouquet.

Now that you've conquered your first lilac, make another. You'll be amazed at the difference in time it takes to make a second one, not to mention how much happier you'll be with the end result. For your third bloom, grab a friend or two and work together!

TIERED GARLAND ORNAMENT

by Patricia Zapata

The repetition of geometric shapes is an ideal way to create visual impact. Trying this with an ornament is simple and it's easy to duplicate as many times as you wish. The tutorial calls for six layers of paper discs, but make more to transform it into an eye-catching garland. Variations in color and texture make the possibilities innumerable.

SUPPLIES AND TOOLS

Tracing paper
Pencil
Cardstock white, 2 sheets,
   8½ x 11 inches (22 x 28 cm)
Disc template (page 109)
Scissors or craft knife
Self-healing cutting mat
Piercer or pushpin
Quilling tool
Ruler
Glue
Twine or embroidery floss
Sewing needle optional

Patricia Zapata

Patricia is a graphic designer and crafter who lives in Texas with her husband and two children. She runs A Little Hut, a paper goods business, and writes a well-known craft blog by the same name. Patricia is the author of *Home, Paper, Scissors: Decorative Paper Accessories for the Home* (Potter Craft, 2009) and a contributor to several design and craft books. Her work has been featured in a variety of online publications such as *Craft, Décor8, Design Sponge, Apartment Therapy*, and many others.

Website: alittlehut.com

Why Paper?

I've been drawn to paper for as long as I can remember. I collected pads when I was a little girl and there was nothing as exciting as a new notebook. As a graphic designer, I renewed my focus on paper because it was always available to me and because it was an easy way to quickly practice and enjoy some handcrafting techniques. I think the thing that keeps me interested in working with paper is its flexible, yet delicate, quality–there's always something new to try and explore.

Tips!

Consider the use of this ornament as a stacked group on a long strand or hung individually as a mobile. Alternating colors of paper would add another level of interest. Additional ideas would be to use discs that diminish or grow in size on each level and/or use beads instead of quilled strips of paper between the discs.

HOW TO MAKE THE TIERED GARLAND ORNAMENT

STEP 1 Trace the disc template onto tracing paper. Transfer the design to the cardstock six times by photocopy or by cutting out the traced image and using it as a template. Make sure to mark the center of each traced image and the markings on the ends of each of the rays.

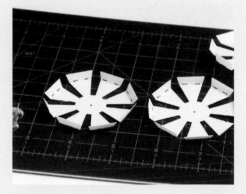

STEP 2 Cut out all six discs. Crease and fold (90-degree angle) the outermost ¼ inch (6 mm) of each ray in the same direction. Poke a hole in the center of each disc using a paper piercer or push pin. Set aside.

STEP 3 Cut six strips of cardstock that measure 7 x ½ inches (18 cm x 13 mm).

STEP 4 Use a quilling tool to roll each strip. Seal the end with a dot of glue. Be careful not to make the rolls too tight, as twine or embroidery floss will be threaded through the center of each roll.

STEP 5 Cut a 10-inch (25 cm) strand of twine or floss and tie a knot on one end. Starting with a disc, alternately thread all six discs and six rolls on the twine, adding a bit of glue between each disc and roll. Be sure to alternate the positions of the disc rays from one layer to the next. Use a needle if it makes this step easier. Make a loop on the end of the twine and use it to hang the ornament.

CITRUS SLICE COASTERS

by Casey Starks

These playful citrus coasters would be great for a summer barbeque.
Your guests could even take them home as party favors. Once you get
the feel for the technique, reuse the supplies to create customized screen
printed coasters for any theme. Try out the herringbone or ikat designs
included in the templates section or come up with your own designs!

There are many different methods for screen printing. The drawing
fluid method, outlined here, allows you to paint a design directly on the
screen. With this technique you can create a beautiful, hand-painted
design and print it on anything, over and over again, in any color. Since
each brushstroke is unique, your design will certainly be one of a kind.

Casey Starks

California native Casey Starks
is the creative mind behind her
brands Vitamini and Vitamod-
ern that feature screen printed
gifts and stationery based on her
original drawings and papercut
designs. When she's not at her
day job as a landscape architect,
Casey can be found blogging,
thrifting, or cruising around Sili-
con Valley in her yellow MINI
Cooper, looking for inspiration.
She loves bright colors, graphic
patterns, and everything retro.

Blog: vitaminihandmade.
blogspot.com
Shop: vitamini.etsy.com and
vitamodern.etsy.com

Why Screen Printing?

Screen printing, also known as silk screening, is an artistic technique that has been around for
centuries. Basically, a screen print is a design that has been created by forcing ink through a
stretched fabric stencil. There are countless methods for creating screen stencils. The most
temporary stencils can be made by applying paper, tape, or contact paper tape directly to the
screen, blocking out the design. The drawing fluid method, outlined in this tutorial, begins with
a hand-painted design applied to the screen as a resist. The open areas are blocked with screen
filler and the design is washed out, resulting in a stencil of the painted design. This is a good
method to start with as a beginner. When I create screens for my business-related prints, I use
the photo emulsion method. With this method, a light-sensitive screen is created. The design,
an opaque, black image on a transparency, is layered over the screen and exposed to light.
The exposed areas of the screen harden, and the spaces underneath the design remain water
soluble. The screen is rinsed and only the design washes out, resulting in a stencil that is an
exact replica of the original design. Preparing a screen for printing can be a labor-intensive
process, but the high-quality printed results, combined with the ease of reproduction, make
the preparation worthwhile.

I fell in love with screen printing because everything about it is fundamentally handmade:
from stretching the screen fabric, to coating the screen, and later applying my own hand drawn
design, and rinsing it out at just the right moment. I also love the professional, high-quality
results. Screen printed designs can be very versatile, in that they can be simple, one color
designs or complex, layered images created with multiple colors and textures. With a screen
print, each color is printed one at a time, so prints with multiple colors are the result of multiple
screen stencils layered over one another. It's an involved process that requires dedication, skill,
and a commitment to the craft. Screen prints also have unique qualities and textures that can't
be achieved with a commercial inkjet or laser printer. For all of these reasons, I find screen
printing to be very addictive. Once I get going, I want to print on everything in sight!

Tip!
Although the ink does wash out eventually, it's usually recommended to wear gloves to reduce the clean up effort.

SUPPLIES AND TOOLS

Screen printing screen pre-stretched with fabric – find these at art stores or get them in the Speedball kit. There are also many tutorials online for making your own screens.

Blue painter's tape 1 inch (2.5 cm) wide

Pencil

Design templates (page 108)

Paintbrushes sizes #1 and #6

Rubber spatula or plastic spoon

Wooden stir sticks

Paper plate

Speedball drawing fluid and screen filler – these come together in a kit

Squeegee

Cardboard strips 2, approximately 8 to 10 inches x 2 inches (20 to 25 cm x 5 cm)

Water-based screen printing inks intended for use on paper (Versatex—non-toxic, permanent, lightfast) Color(s) of choice; I mixed red and white to get grapefruit pink.

Small container with a lid if you are mixing your own ink colors

Paper coasters 4 inch diameter (10 cm) find these on Etsy.com in the supplies section

Scrap paper to protect your work surface and for test prints

Speedball Speed Clean (not pictured) for reclaiming your screen when you are done with your stencil

Apron (not pictured)

Latex gloves (not pictured)

HOW TO MAKE THE SCREEN

Tips!
Protect your work surface with paper, taping down the edges. Put on an apron to protect your clothes. Read the instructions on the drawing fluid and screen filler. Follow all safety precautions stated on the labels.

STEP 1 Position the screen over one or more of the design templates. Using a pencil, trace the design onto the screen fabric. This outline will be a guide when painting the screen to create the stencil.

STEP 2 Tape off edges of the screen with painter's tape. Add two strips of tape along the right side of the screen. The tape will keep the drawing fluid from bleeding to the edge of the screen and will make it easier to clean.

STEP 3 Prop up the edges of the screen so the fabric isn't resting on the tabletop. Use two books or two blocks of wood.

STEP 4 Stir the drawing fluid with a stirring stick and dip the paintbrush into it. Following the pencil lines, paint the design onto the screen. Reload the brush often and make sure the brush strokes are solid. The design that is painted will create the stencil, so anything painted with the drawing fluid will be printed. Don't paint the outline of the coaster. This line will be used later to line up the prints. If the design isn't coming out as intended, simply rinse it out in the sink with cold water, let the screen dry, and start over.

STEP 5 Keeping the screen in a horizontal position, let the painted design dry for about an hour. The drawing fluid is dry when it's not tacky to the touch. **STEP 6** Once the design is dry, follow the instructions on the bottle of screen filler. Stir it slowly with a stir stick or a plastic spoon to prevent bubbles that could make holes in the filler. Use a rubber spatula to scoop the screen filler onto the top of the screen over the top two layers of tape. Spread it across in a line.

STEP 7 Holding the squeegee at a 45-degree angle, press it to the screen above the screen filler. Slowly pull the squeegee across the screen, spreading the screen filler over your design all the way to the other end of the screen. It is best to do this in one solid motion, as multiple passes with the squeegee may begin to dissolve the design. If there are open spots in the screen filler, paint them in with a brush after the first coat has dried.

STEP 8 Keeping the screen in a horizontal position let the painted design dry completely, about an hour. Set a fan nearby on low to speed drying time. **STEP 9** Hold the screen up to the light to check for holes. If there are any open spaces in the screen filler, use a paintbrush to fill them in with screen filler. Let dry.

STEP 10 When the screen filler is dry to the touch and the screen is all filled in, it's time to rinse! Pull off the painter's tape. Set the screen in the sink and rinse both sides with cold water. Don't use hot water as it could remove the screen filler. Concentrate the water on the painted design. The blue drawing fluid will begin to wash away. Continue to rinse the screen until the entire design has been dissolved. When all of the blue drawing fluid is gone, let the screen dry. The screen is ready to print!

HOW TO PRINT THE COASTERS

STEP 1 Tape off the edges of the screen again, this time on the underside overlapping the edge of the screen filler. Any part of the screen not filled with the red screen filler or tape may transfer ink onto the work surface, so if there are other gaps in the screen filler that were missed, cover them on the underside of the screen with tape.

STEP 2 Prep the work surface for printing. Tape one strip of cardboard onto the paper-covered surface vertically to the left of the screen and one horizontally above the screen. When you are printing, the screen will be lined up to these edges.

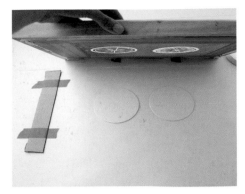

STEP 3a With the screen lined up with the cardboard strips, place two of the coasters under the screen in the approximate area of the two designs.

STEP 3b Looking through the screen, move the coasters until they line up with the pencil outlines and the designs are centered.

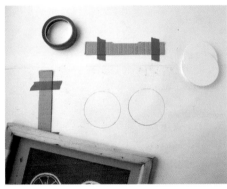

STEP 3c Once the coasters are in the right place, pick up the screen and trace their outlines onto the paper work surface. These outlines will guide you where to place the coasters when printing so the design will be centered. In screen printing, this is called registration.

STEP 4 Move the coasters aside. Place a scrap piece of paper down, and put the screen back in place, aligned with the cardboard strips.

STEP 5 Prepare the ink. Use the ink colors straight out of the jar or mix your own. Scoop the ink out and onto the top of the screen right above the designs. A little goes a long way.

STEP 6 Place the squeegee onto the screen above the ink. Holding it at a 45-degree angle, pull the squeegee toward you, spreading the ink over the screen and through the stencil. Keeping the ink in front of the squeegee, pull it across the screen two or three times to ensure even coverage. Lift the screen and remove the test print. Repeat the process a few more times with scrap paper until the test prints are solid and consistent.

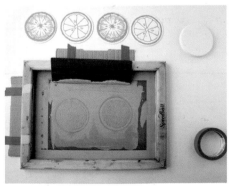

STEP 7 Place the blank paper coasters in their outlined spots, and repeat. Work quickly so the ink doesn't dry on the screen. **STEP 8** When the printing is done, scoop the excess ink back into the container, remove the tape, and wash both sides of the screen with cold water to remove the leftover ink. Let dry. The stencil will remain on the screen until it is removed with Speedball Speed Clean, so repeat the process with different colors!

Tips!

Try printing on other paper products like note cards, post-cards, party invitations, wrapping paper, etc. The same equipment and screen may be used to print on fabric as well; just make sure to use inks intended for fabrics. Wash out the screen with Speedball Speed Clean and start over with a new design.

Since this design applies to a few different citrus fruits, try printing with orange, lime green, or lemon yellow ink.

STICKY NOTES NOTEPAD HOLDER

by Stefani Tadio

This Sticky Notes Notepad Holder combines pretty with practical. The hand stitched, beaded cover holds a three-inch (7.6 cm) square, self-adhesive notepad that can be replaced over and over again.

Stefani Tadio

A paper artist in the beautiful Finger Lakes region of upstate New York, Stefani's specialty is hand stitched, original designs on paper. She creates patterns on a computer and stitches by hand, one stitch at a time, to make framed art, sticky notes, greeting cards, wearable art pins, magnets, decorative tins, and hanging ornaments. Her work is available at area festivals, local stores, and in her online shop.

Website: pinetreedesigns.com

Why Paper?

I think I've always been drawn to paper because I remember that shopping for school supplies was the best day ever each year. In the mid-90s I took a rubber stamping class and my passion for paper skyrocketed. I like that it's an inexpensive and portable medium, but mostly I love that paper is available in an enormous range of colors and textures. I love color!

I've worked with a needle and thread since I was a teenager when Mom taught my sister and me to needlepoint. I've also quilted and cross-stitched quite a bit, so when I first saw paper embroidery patterns online, it was the perfect combination for me. Combining my own designs with the huge range of colors in paper and thread makes the possibilities limitless.

SUPPLIES AND TOOLS

Cardstock black, turquoise, dark gold, 1 sheet of each color, 8½ x 11 inches (22 x 28 cm), use highest quality available

Copy paper white, 1 sheet, 8½ x 11 inches (22 x 28 cm)

Stitching hole template (page 109)

Stitching and beading diagram (page 30)

Polyester thread dark orange, 1 yard (1 m) (Coats & Clark 40 wt Trilobal Polyester #300A)

Polyester thread turquoise, 3 yards (2.75 meters) (Coats & Clark 40 wt Trilobal Polyester #356)

Variegated thread orange/turquoise, 3 yards (2.75 meters) (Madeira 40 wt PolyNeon #1600)

Note: These threads may be located in the machine embroidery area of a fabric store. Other polyester or silk threads may be substituted.

Copy machine

Ruler

Pencil

Scissors

Craft punches

    1-inch (2.5 cm) diameter 8-petal daisy punch

    ½-inch (13 mm) diameter 8-petal daisy punch

    ¼-inch (6 mm) diameter 8-petal daisy punch

    2½-inch (6.5 cm) circle punch

    3-inch (7.6 cm) scalloped circle punch

Scalloped-edge scissors if scalloped circle punch is not available

Compass if a scalloped circle punch is not available

Needle tool or pushpin

Soft surface pad of paper or thick mouse pad

Cellophane tape

Sewing needle as small as you are comfortable using

Seed beads turquoise, size 15, quantity 32

Beading needle

Small plate or piece of felt to hold beads during beading process

Bone folder (or pen without ink) to score fold lines

White crafting glue

Crystal one, topaz, size 09, flat back

Notepad self-adhesive, 3 inches (7.6 cm) square

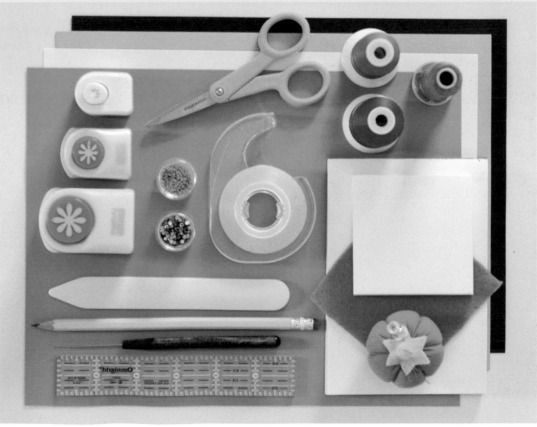

HOW TO DO THE STITCHING

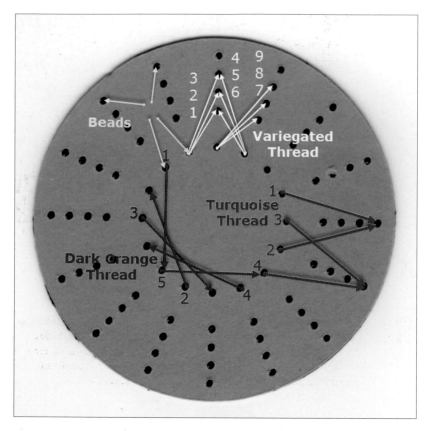

STEP 1 Use the 3-inch (7.6 cm) scalloped circle punch to punch a turquoise scalloped circle. Set aside. If the punch is not available, lightly draw a 3-inch (7.6 cm) circle with a compass and carefully cut it out with scalloped-edge scissors. Erase the pencil line. **STEP 2** Make a photocopy of the 2½-inch (6.5 cm) stitching holes template onto white copy paper. Punch out the template or cut it with scissors. **STEP 3** Use the 2½-inch (6.5 cm) circle punch to punch a black cardstock circle. If the punch is not available, trace the 2½-inch (6.5 cm) stitching holes template on black cardstock and cut it out. **STEP 4** Lay the 2½-inch (6.5 cm) stitching holes template on top of the black circle and tape both to a soft surface, such as a pad of paper or thick mouse pad. Use a needle tool or pushpin to poke through the template markings, creating the stitching and beading holes in the black cardstock. **STEP 5** Carefully remove the template and hold the black cardstock circle up to the light to check for missed holes. **STEP 6** Working with a comfortable length of variegated thread, tape one end to the back of the black circle. Thread the other end through the needle. **STEP 7** Coming up from the back, bring the threaded needle through the cardstock at one of the innermost holes. Go back down through the closest hole to the upper right. Come back up through the original hole and down through the next hole in that row. Refer to numbered steps on the stitching and beading diagram to the left. **STEP 8** Complete the variegated stitching in the same manner around the circle until completed. Start and end thread by taping it to the back of the black circle. **STEP 9** Work with turquoise thread to stitch the holes around the perimeter of the black cardstock, using the same innermost and outermost holes in accordance with the stitching diagram.

STEP 10 The last stitching step is to use the dark orange thread to create the spirelli design in the center. Starting at one of the innermost holes, come up through that hole, count past three holes counterclockwise and go down through the fourth hole. Come up at the next counterclockwise hole, skip three clockwise holes, and go down through the fourth hole, which is next to the first starting hole. Repeat these steps as guided by the diagram (up at numbers, down at arrows) until spirelli is complete.

Tips!
Use as small a needle as possible to keep the holes tiny and unobtrusive.

The key to perfect, flat stitches is to hold the thread taut on the back of the paper as the next stitch is started.

A beading needle is very thin and has an eye that is tiny enough to go through the holes of the selected beads.

The needle tool is more comfortable to hold, but a pushpin may provide better control.

To cut smoothly, hold scissors steady while turning the paper.

HOW TO DO THE BEADING AND ASSEMBLY

STEP 1 Thread the beading needle with the same color thread as the beads. (Turquoise for this example.) **STEP 2** Pour the beads onto a small plate or piece of felt to prevent them from rolling around the work surface.

STEP 3 Tape one end of the thread to the back of the black circle. Come up through one of the innermost holes (which will already have many threads in it from the previous steps) and pick up one of the seed beads. Let it slide down the thread to the cardstock. Insert the needle back down through the same hole (but not through the bead again) and pull it taut. See bead placement steps on stitching and beading diagram.

STEP 4 Cut a piece of dark gold cardstock that measures 7 x 3¹/₄ inches (17.8 x 8.3 cm). **STEP 5** Use a ruler to measure from the short end toward the center 3¹/₄ inches (8.3 cm) and mark twice lightly with a pencil. Repeat from the other short end toward the center. **STEP 6** On each end, line the ruler up with the two pencil marks and score the width of the paper with the bone folder. Fold the paper on these lines, straightening the paper if the lines are not perfectly straight. After each end is folded, a half-inch spine will have been created in the center of the 7-inch (17.8 cm) cover.
STEP 7 Apply glue to the back of the stitched and beaded black circle, particularly around the outer edge where there is less stitching. There is no need to cover the entire back with glue and don't allow it to seep through the stitching holes. **STEP 8** Glue the black circle to the center of the turquoise scalloped circle, applying firm pressure until the glue sets.

STEP 9 Apply glue to the back of the turquoise scalloped circle, again paying close attention to the outermost edge. Glue this circle to the center of one half of the dark gold cover, using firm pressure until the glue sets.
STEP 10 Tear the paper backing off the self-adhesive notepad. Apply glue to the back of the notepad at the top edge and along the spine. Place the pad in the cover; apply firm pressure to both the spine and back until all is secure. **STEP 11** For the center embellishment, use the 1-inch (25 mm) 8-petal daisy punch to create a daisy from one of the papers used in this project or favorite paper scrap. Glue it in the center of the spirelli stitching. Use contrasting papers to do the same with the ¹/₂-inch (13 mm) 8-petal daisy punch, and the ¹/₄-inch (6 mm) 8-petal daisy punch. Glue the daisies directly on top of one another, petals aligned or each layer turned slightly, as in the example. Glue the small topaz crystal to the center of the ¹/₂-inch (13 mm) daisy.

MYSTERIOUS STATIONERY BOX

by Cecelia Louie

When first introduced to the Japanese KARAKURI BAKO or "trick box" with its two openings, I was instantly fascinated. Traditionally made of wood and fabric, the box is commonly used to hold jewelry in evenly divided compartments. I wondered how it would fare as a stationery holder and determined that by moving the dividers to accommodate pens and pencils in the large central area, the smaller end compartments would now be ideal for Post-it Notes and paper clips.

Using the right materials is key in this adapted-to-paper project. The binder's board is acid-free and warp-resistant. As the glue dried, I discovered that the slight bowing would flatten itself perfectly. I used a rotary cutter to ensure my cuts were 90° and consistent, but an X-ACTO knife may certainly be used instead.

The high quality solid and printed handmade Japanese papers I chose to cover the box contain long pulp fibers that make them able to withstand creasing and repeated handling. Because the patterned paper was a single-sided print, it was necessary to glue two pieces back-to-back for the hinge section. The paper was thick enough to prevent the glue from seeping through, yet yielded enough to be manipulated around the board edges without cracking or buckling. As with the binder board, the slight warping caused by glue application disappeared as it dried.

Making a mock-up with inexpensive paper and mat board to fully understand all of the components and how they fit is a good step to take before cutting high-end materials. Practice makes perfect holds true with this project, and the sharp edges and clean folds in the final piece speak volumes when completed.

Cecelia Louie

A graduate of Emily Carr College of Art and Design, Vancouver, BC, Cecelia Louie is a graphic designer by day and a paper crafter by night. She is a contributing author of *The New Encyclopedia of Origami & Papercraft Techniques* [Running Press, 2011]. To view more of her work, please visit **craftingcreatures.blogspot.com**

Why Paper?
My first love of paper began with the folding of an origami balloon at the impressionable age of 7. That pivotal introduction ignited an appetite to create and re-create ideas from paper, developing into a lifelong love affair."

Visit tuttlepublishing.com to view a short video that demonstrates the trick of the stationery box.

SUPPLIES AND TOOLS

Millboard $\frac{1}{16}$ inch (1.6 mm) thick; I used Lineco Binder's Board 0.067 inch (1.7 mm)

Decorative papers 2, preferably with long pulp fibers

The papers used here are:

a) Savoir-Faire Hana Yuzen Indigo - handmade, silk screened paper, Pattern: Flower Blooms #95-5187 Sources: savoirfaire.com and paperya.ca

b) Hanji (Korean mulberry paper) deep blue

X-ACTO knife (rotary cutter optional)

Pencil

Ruler

Glue I used Lineco Neutral pH Adhesive (fine-tip bottle, if possible)

Paintbrush

Sandpaper

Bone folder

Awl

HOW TO MAKE THE BOX BOTTOM

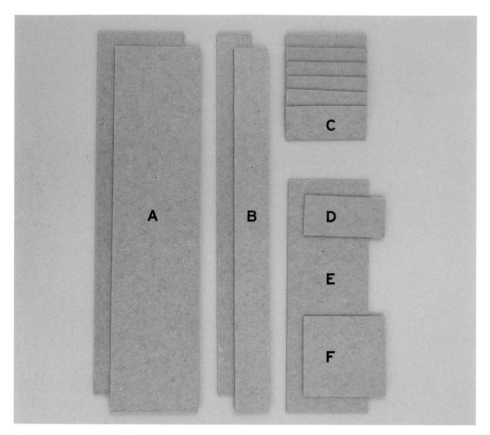

STEP 1 Using a fine tip glue bottle, glue one length to the bottom.

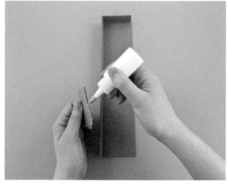

STEP 2 Glue the widths, then the final length. Use a straight edge or box to keep the edges and sides aligned as the glue sets.

BOX PANELS Cut the following pieces using millboard:
A. 2 pieces (top and bottom) 2¹/₂ x 11 inches (6.35 x 27.9 cm)
B. 2 pieces (lengths) 1 x 11 inches (2.54 x 27.9 cm)
C. 6 pieces (widths) 2³/₈ x 1 inches (6.03 x 2.54 cm)
D. 1 piece (locking piece 1) 2³/₈ x 1 inches (6.03 x 2.54 cm)
E. 1 piece (locking piece 2) 2³/₈ x 7 inches (6.03 x 17.9 cm)
F. 1 piece (locking piece 3) 2³/₈ x 2³/₈ inches (6.03 x 6.03 cm)

Tips!

Lineco millboard is sold in packages of 4 sheets; each measures 15 x 20¹/₂ inches (38 x 52 cm). One sheet is enough to make the box.

The patterned and solid handmade papers are sold as 24 x 36-inch (61 x 91 cm) sheets. One sheet of each is enough.

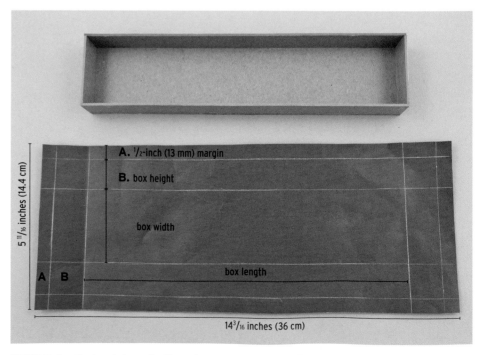

5¹¹/₁₆ inches (14.4 cm)

A. ¹/₂-inch (13 mm) margin

B. box height

box width

A   B

box length

14³/₁₆ inches (36 cm)

STEP 3 Use the box to trace its dimensions on your paper (white pencil crayon is used here for photo purposes only). The following two photos show further detail.

STEP 4 Flip the box on its sides and bottom to trace heights and mark the dimensions, allowing 1/2-inch (13 mm) margin from all four sides.

STEP 5 Using the box to mark your lines saves time from having to measure every panel with a ruler.

STEP 6 Lay the box on its length against the first line. Place a ruler on the inside of the box and mark the edge of the paper.

STEP 7 Connect the edge marking to the intersecting lines (corner) to create a tapered tab. Repeat with the three opposing corners.

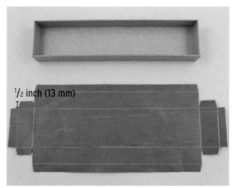

STEP 8 Measure a 1/2-inch (13 mm) tab for the width of the box. Taper the tab. Repeat with the three opposing corners. Cut along the markings.

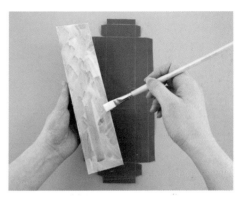

STEP 9 Using a brush, apply a thin, even layer of glue to the bottom surface of the box.

STEP 10 Place the box within the markings. Turn over and gently flatten the surface with a bone folder to squeeze out any air bubbles or pockets of excess glue.

STEP 11 Apply glue to the box width tabs and flatten the paper over the rim, sides, and inside the box.

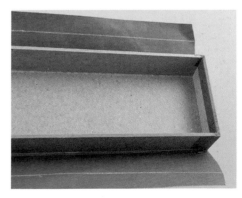

STEP 12 There will be some buckling at the top corners; just flatten the paper as it softens with the glue's moisture. Excess paper will overflow past the inside corners, ensuring a good overlap to hide the millboard. Repeat for the opposite side.

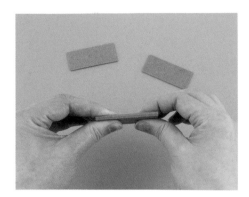

STEP 13 Pair up and glue the remaining four width pieces to create the compartment dividers.

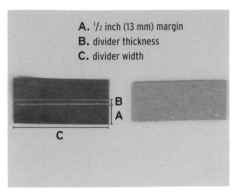

A. ½ inch (13 mm) margin
B. divider thickness
C. divider width

STEP 14 Cut the paper as shown with a ½-inch (13 mm) margin on either side.

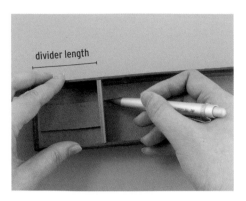

divider length

STEP 15 Place one divider inside the box, using its 2⅜-inch (6.03 cm) length as a guide, and pencil mark a square compartment.

divider width

STEP 16 Repeat on the opposite end, using the 1-inch (2.54 cm) width as a guide, marking the smallest compartment.

STEP 17 Glue the dividers in the box.

STEP 18 Apply glue to the divider's cover, matching up the lines, then flatten the paper over both sides.

HOW TO COVER THE BOTTOM INTERIOR

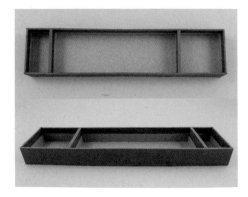

Box bottom with dividers

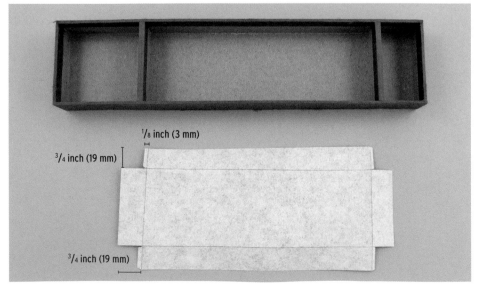

⅛ inch (3 mm)

¾ inch (19 mm)

¾ inch (19 mm)

STEP 1 Measure the inside dimensions of the compartments and draw a replica on the second sheet of decorative paper. Add ¾ inch (19 mm) on all four sides. Add ⅛-inch (3 mm) tapered tabs on the lengths. Cut the paper.

STEP 2 Apply glue to the compartment bottom.

STEP 3 Flatten the paper along the bottom. Expect the tabs to buckle a little.

STEP 4 Fold down the widths to get them temporarily out of the way. Place a scrap piece of paper inside the compartment to shield the area as glue is applied to the tab. Flatten the paper.

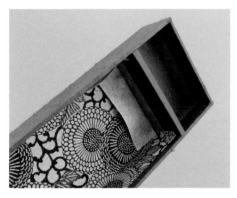

STEP 5 The length's tab should overflow past the corner to hide all millboard and add strength to the joins.

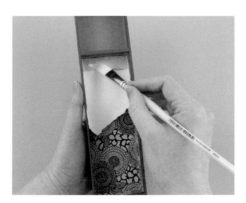

STEP 6 Shield the compartment as glue is applied to the width tabs.

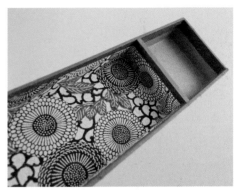

STEP 7 Flatten the paper against the box. Repeat for remaining compartments.

STEP 8 Using an awl in the tight corners will help maneuver the tabs in place.

STEP 9 You can use a bone folder or paint brush handle to smooth out the material.

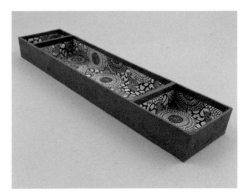

Finished box bottom

HOW TO MAKE THE BOX LID

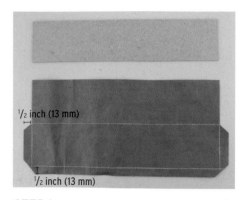

STEP 1 Trace the lid on the paper. Add ½ inch (13 mm) on three sides. Trace the lid again along the length as the fourth tab. Trim a 45-degree triangle from the corners, just outside the juxtaposed corner lines.

½ inch (13 mm)

½ inch (13 mm)

STEP 2 Glue the lid to the first traced rectangle. Glue the widths first, pressing the corner excess onto the lengths. Repeat with the two remaining tabs.

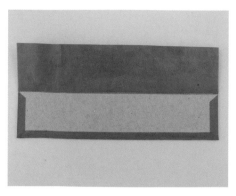

STEP 3 Gluing the fourth tab completes the lid.

HOW TO MAKE THE HINGE

STEP 1 Measuring from the middle of the dividers to achieve the widths, cut 3 strips of paper, 9 inches (22.9 cm) in length.

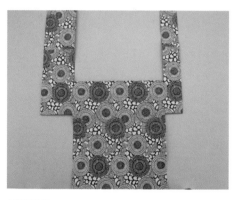

STEP 2 Glue the two small hinges to the lid. Glue the middle hinge in the opposite direction. Flip over.

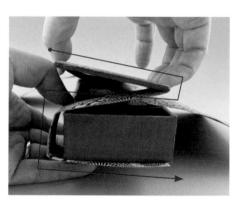

STEP 3 Wrap each strip around and under the lid, creasing sharply along the corners. Continue wrapping around the box bottom, creating a zig zag shape with the strips.

Tip!
The hinge wraps around the lid and box, exposing both sides of the paper. If the patterned paper is single-sided, pour glue near one edge and spread quickly with a stiff card. Put the backs together and flatten immediately. Allow to dry before proceeding.

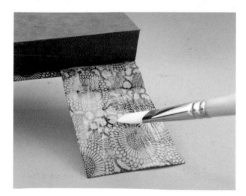

STEP 4 Glue the strip to the box side and bottom only. Repeat for remaining two strips to finish the two-way hinges.

STEP 5 Trim away the excess by following the side of the box with an X-ACTO knife.

STEP 6 The glue is applied on the panels shown with a red asterisk (*).

HOW TO MAKE THE LOCKING PIECES

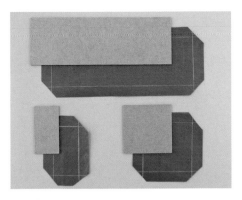

STEP 1 Trace the pieces onto the paper, leaving ½ inch (13 mm) on all sides. Trim a 45-degree triangle from all corners. Do not glue yet!

STEP 2 Stack some items inside the compartment, leaving just enough room for the locking pieces to lie flush against the lid.

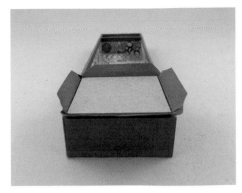

STEP 3 The locking pieces need to be friction fitted. If they are too tight, use sandpaper to shave down the edges until a snug fit is achieved.

STEP 4 Glue the paper to the locking piece.

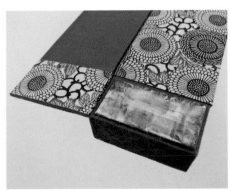

STEP 5 Apply glue to the locking piece and close the lid.

Tip!
Using too much glue may cause the excess to seep over the sides.

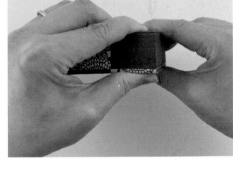

STEP 6 Press tightly for a few minutes to allow the glue to set. Gently open and clean off any excess glue. Close the lid. Set a heavy object on top and allow the glue to dry completely. Repeat for the other compartments.

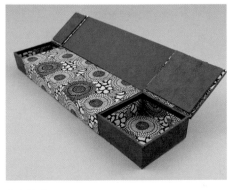

STEP 7 Open the lid from the left to expose the two smaller compartments.

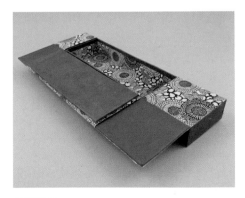

STEP 8 Open the lid from the right to expose the main compartment.

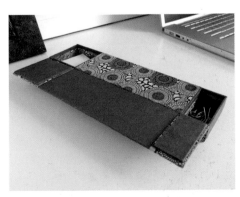

DONE Enjoy hiding secrets in the mystery box.

SILHOUETTE PORTRAIT ART

by Lorraine Nam

Silhouette paper cutting by hand originated in the early 1700s and was extremely popular in the 1800s. The use of a profile photograph has certainly simplified the process! Even a novice crafter will be able to produce a modern silhouette that will look lovely when framed for display in any room. Make one for every member of your family or give your friends their silhouettes as personalized gifts.

Lorraine Nam

Lorraine cuts, slashes, and dissects paper to create intricate cut paper images. Her work has appeared nationwide in publications such as *Papercraft 2*, *Bitch Magazine*, the *Women in Film International Short Film Festival* (WIFI), and has been shown in Drift Gallery in Kittery, Maine. She currently resides in Brooklyn, New York as a textile designer and freelance illustrator.

Website: lorrainenam.com

SUPPLIES AND TOOLS

Cardstock white, 2 sheets, 8½ x 11 inches (22 x 28 cm)
Cardstock black, 1 sheet, 8½ x 11 inches (22 x 28 cm)
Rice paper 1 sheet, 8½ x 11 inches (22 x 28 cm)
Copy paper 1 sheet, 8½ x 11 inches (22 x 28 cm)
Photograph
Scissors
Craft knife #11 (X-ACTO)
Printer
Pencil
Eraser
Glue stick
Self-healing cutting mat thick cardboard also works well
Tape **optional**
Oval template (page 110)
Flower template A (page 110)
Flower template B (page 111)

"Why Paper?

I've always been drawn to paper and its qualities of strength and purity. I went through different processes of manipulating paper and became particularly infatuated with cutting paper. I started cutting paper to simplify my drawings... lines became one and I was interested in what emerged. Light and shadow were also important in my work, and cast shadow became a particular obsession of mine. It provided depth in my pieces despite the flatness of cut paper."

HOW TO MAKE THE SILHOUETTE

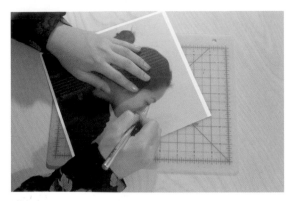

STEP 1 Take a photograph of the subject in profile or use an existing photograph. **STEP 2** Print out the photograph onto an 8½ x 11-inch (22 x 28 cm) piece of copy paper, making sure the silhouette will fit inside the Oval Template. **STEP 3** Carefully cut out the profile using scissors or a craft knife. Be sure to get the curves and hair just right— that's what makes it look just like the person! Don't worry too much about the rest of the body; cut off the silhouette below the shoulders.

STEP 4 Remove the Oval Template page from the book and cut out the oval. Use scissors for the outer edge of the oval if that is easier, but use the craft knife to cut out the inner space of the oval.

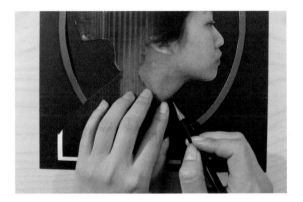

STEP 5 Position the cut oval in the center of the black cardstock and trace around both the outer and inner lines.

STEP 6 Position the silhouette in relation to the oval on the black cardstock, making sure the shoulders or hair connects to the bottom of the oval. Carefully trace with a pencil and set the photo and oval aside.

STEP 7 Cut out the traced silhouette and the oval from the black paper, making sure the oval is connected to the silhouette. There's the first layer!

Tips!
Position the subject against a simple background. A three quarter or side profile view works best.

HOW TO MAKE THE FLORAL BACKGROUND

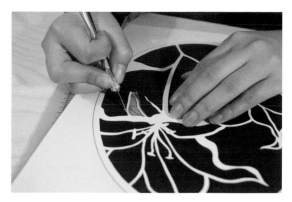

STEP 1 Remove Flower Template A from the book and using a craft knife, slowly cut out the flower petals. Relax the wrists and apply just light pressure on the knife to prevent accidentally cutting off any details. Don't worry if it happens—that's what the tape is for! Place the template onto a white piece of cardstock and trace. Use the craft knife to cut it out again.

STEP 2 Remove Flower Template B from book and carefully cut it out. **STEP 3** Trace the template onto a separate sheet of white cardstock and cut out the traced outline. This takes a while, but it's worth it!

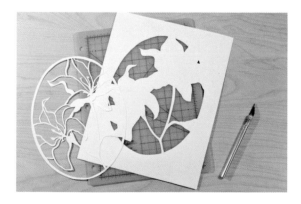

STEP 4 Place Flower Template B on top of Flower Template A. Make sure the edges of Template A do not peek out from Template B. If they show, carefully trim them.

FINISHING TOUCHES

STEP 1 Position all of the layers onto a sheet of rice paper. On top should be the silhouette, then Flower Template B, below that is Flower Template A, and on the bottom is the rice paper. **STEP 2** Make small, light pencil marks on each sheet to show where to place the silhouette on each layer. **STEP 3** Lift the silhouette and apply glue to the back, making sure to cover the edges. **STEP 4** Place the silhouette carefully onto the next layer and wipe away any excess glue. **STEP 5** Keep applying glue to the layers until all are glued together. **STEP 6** Allow the glue to dry for a few minutes and erase any stray pencil marks. **STEP 7** Place in a frame and hang!

Tips!

Always cut the templates and paper layers on the self-healing cutting mat to avoid damaging the work surface.

While making the cuts, hold the paper with the opposite hand for more control. Rotate the paper as needed.

For curves: Do them gradually. Don't try to cut a long curve, as it's easy to veer off and make a mistake. Instead, go slowly and make shorter cuts.

Play around with a variety of colored layers or patterned papers.

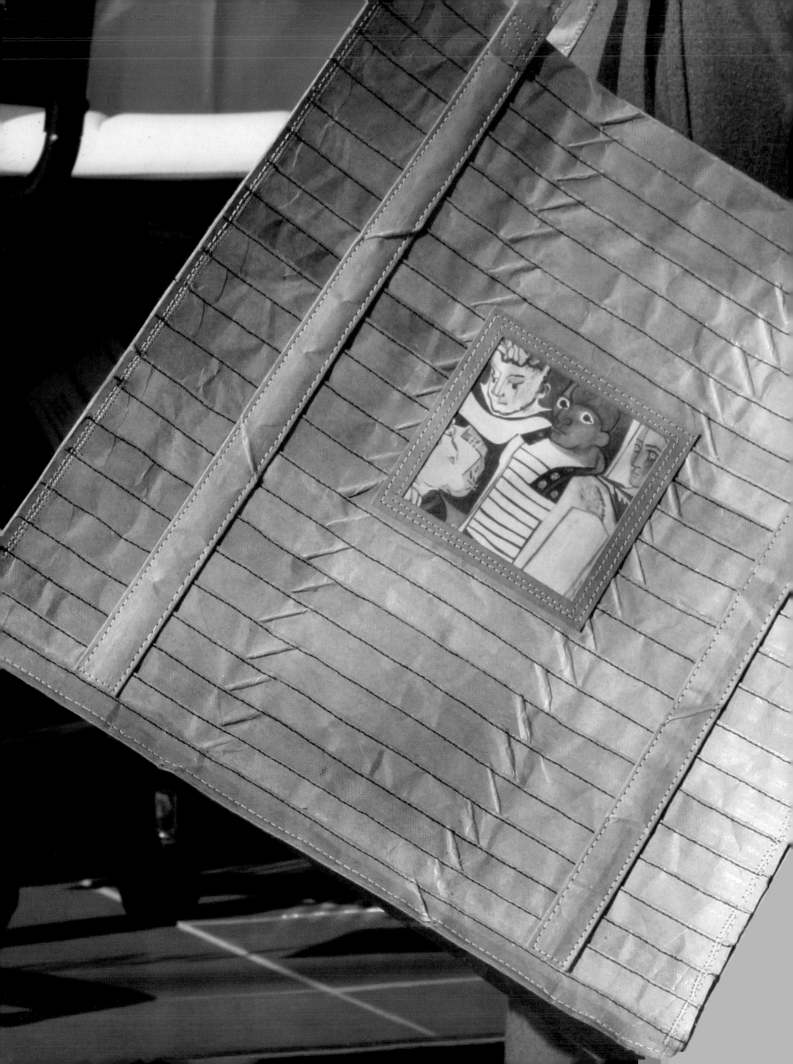

CHAPTER 2

FASHION ACCESSORIES

Make a stylish tote from a surprising material and experiment with water-colors on fibrous paper to create a pretty fascinator.

TIGER LILY FASCINATOR

by Danielle Connel

A tropical flower handmade by you! This beautiful hair accessory showcases the rich colors of a tiger lily with no worry of wilting or fading. And why stop with just one? Use the techniques you'll learn here to create lilies in whatever colors you love. Wear this flower as a fascinator or corsage, or fasten a few to a headband.

Danielle Connel

Danielle designs paper flowers at her messy desk in Houston, Texas. A mother of three, she has long been drawn to the endless possibilities of paper crafting. She enjoys creating both literal and whimsical interpretations of flowers. Her work has been cherished by many brides. Danielle can be found via her Etsy shop, **shinymonkeybuttons.etsy.com**

Tips!
Don't be afraid to make the fascinator your own. Add other flowers, decorative buttons, and try different color combinations.

Have patience! Let your creation dry overnight before fastening it in your hair.

Why Paper?

If you ask my children why I love paper, they will tell you it started on a dark and stormy night... During a tornado warning, my three daughters and I were waiting out a storm with flashlights in our hallway. Looking for a way to keep everyone distracted, I rummaged in the hall closet and found a kirigami kit we had been given as a gift. By the dim light we cut amazing shapes and patterns! Even after the lights came back on, we stayed where we were until we had cut every design in the booklet.

Only paper gives me the flexibility to fold, cut, and shape the flowers I create. It may seem a bit unusual to trace the progression from kirigami to paper flowers, but to me it makes perfect sense. I design and cut each petal by hand, playing with the cuts until the finished flower looks just so.

SUPPLIES

Mulberry paper white, 2 sheets,
   8½ x 11 inches (22 x 28 cm)
Button 1 inch (2.5 cm) diameter with
   2 fairly large holes
Buttons 4 mini-size, ¼ inch (6 mm)
   diameter with 2 holes
Wrapped-paper floral stem wire white,
   18 gauge
Floral tape white
Tube watercolor paint yellow, orange,
   red
Jaw clip 3-4 inches (7.6 cm-10 cm)
   long
Ribbon organdy that matches jaw clip
   color

TOOLS

Lily petal templates (page 109)
Glue stick tacky (Aleene's
   Tacky Glue Stick)
Craft glue strong (Aleene's
   Original Tacky Glue)
Wire cutters
Pliers
Paintbrush small, flat
Scissors
Pencil
Paper towels
Palette or plate for paint
Jar or glass
Floral foam

HOW TO MAKE THE TIGER LILY

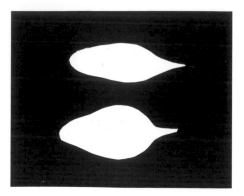

STEP 1a Cut out the two lily petal templates.

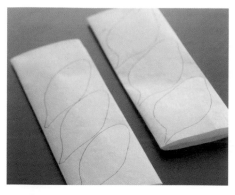

STEP 1b Fold each sheet of mulberry paper widthwise into fourths. Position each petal template on an angle and trace it three times. Hold the layers of paper securely and cut out each tracing. The result will be six pairs of each petal, but only three of each size will be needed to complete a flower. Use the extras to experiment with in step 5.

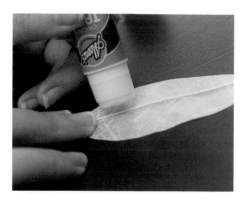

STEP 2 Completely coat one side of one petal of each pair using the tacky glue stick. Place a wire on the petal midline and run the glue stick over the wire.

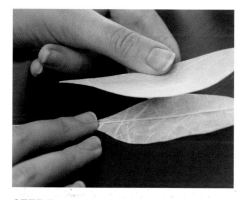

STEP 3 Place a matching petal on top and press them together. Trim edges to eliminate any stray pencil marks and irregularities. Set aside the petal pairs to allow the glue to dry.

STEP 4a Make the button stamens: Fold a piece of floral wire in half to judge the midpoint, and loop it through the large button's holes. Twist the wire around itself snugly against the underside of the button. Cut another wire stem into fourths and repeat this step with each of the mini-buttons. Insert two mini-buttons into each hole of the large button, leaving enough wire for the mini-buttons to stand up and fan out.

STEP 4b Twist the mini-button wires around the main stem. Pliers may be helpful here to twist so many wires. Wrap a 3 or 4-inch (7.6 or 10 cm) piece of floral tape around the twisted wire, pulling and pinching it tightly while wrapping.

STEP 5a Now the painting fun! Squeeze a small amount of red, orange and yellow paint onto the palette or paper plate. Wet each wired petal by immersing it in water.

STEP 5b Stand each petal upright in floral foam throughout the remainder of the process.

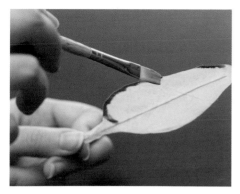

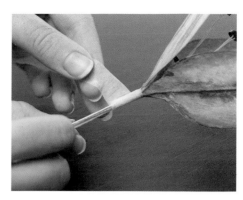

STEP 5c Begin with one of the spare petals. Wet a brush with water and dip it into the orange paint, picking up a brushful of color. Run the brush along the outer edge of the petal. The color should bleed into the paper's fibers. If it doesn't bleed as much as desired, go over the edge with a wet (water) brush. If the color looks too light, pick up more paint and go around the edge again.

STEP 5d After the edges have been painted, use a very wet brush to add a yellow wash over both sides of the entire petal. While everything is still wet, use a medium-diluted red along the bottom edge of the petal and hold it upside down, allowing the color to bleed into the center. Paper towels can be used to blot paint away if the color is too dark.

STEP 6a After the petals have dried for a few hours, assemble the flower: Hold the wider petals around the wire bundle. Wrap floral tape around the petal bases and wire bundle, securing everything together.

STEP 6b Position the narrow petals around the wide petals in the spaces between them.

STEP 6c Firmly wrap all of the wires together with tape. **STEP 6d** Shape the petals by curling the tips back and up.

STEP 7a Measure the stem against the length of the jaw clip. Use the wire cutter to clip off any extra stem.

STEP 7b Run strong craft glue along the top of the clip and bend the flower so that the blossom faces away from the opening. Wrap the stem lightly with floral tape to hold the flower in place while the glue dries.

STEP 7c Wrap ribbon around the clip and stem. Try to do this sparingly so it doesn't interfere with the clip's teeth, but still covers the stem. Glue the ribbon end in an inconspicuous spot.

DONE!

SUPPLIES AND TOOLS

Brown bag handles You'll need about 87 handles
White glue
Cotton thread any color
Self-adhesive clear laminate 1 sheet
Image from magazine/newspaper no bigger than 6 inches (15 cm) square
Cardboard a cereal box panel, for example
Beeswax
Duct tape any color
Paintbrush 1 inch (2.5 cm)
Sewing machine
Scissors
Pencil
Metal ruler with a cork back
Self-healing cutting mat with grid
Binder clips at least 6

EVERYDAY TOTE BAG

by Richela Fabian Morgan

Bags are utilitarian objets d'art, things of beauty that incidentally carry one's personal belongings. And a bag by any other name remains just a bag and yet something more: purse, clutch, satchel, briefcase, or suitcase. These words can relate purpose, size, and sometimes its material. For example, clutches are usually fancy and small, an accessory to an evening gown that glitters or shimmers, constructed with silk or velvet, and encrusted with rhinestones or beads. So what's a tote bag? Tote bags are usually single pocket containers with shoulder straps, meant for precarious stuffing of items large or small, hard or soft, heavy or light. This particular everyday tote bag is made from the handles of brown paper grocery bags, a sturdy material that never seems to get the recognition it deserves. And rubbing a little beeswax on the surface makes it resistant to the elements. Really. This project requires a total of 87 handles from large brown grocery bags. It sounds like a lot to save up, but a few weeks of "forgetting" those reusable shopping bags will yield handles aplenty. A note on sewing paper with a sewing machine: The little bits of paper can jam up the lower chamber. Every so often, take a can of compressed air and clean it out.

Tips!
Protective beeswax gives extra life to brown paper. Simply hold the little brick and rub it directly on the surface like an eraser. It doesn't change the color of the paper, nor does it need to dry after application. Apply the beeswax as the very last step and do so carefully around any stitching where it tends to collect.

Why Paper?
Paper crafting is relatable. You can look at a finished paper project and automatically understand the work that went into achieving it. And it's because as a material, paper is ubiquitous. Every single one of us knows what it feels like, how to fold it, and the strength needed to rip a sheet in half or crumple it up in a ball. The experience of manipulating paper is universal.

I tend to reuse printed material like magazines and newspapers for my craft, but occasionally I can be seen at a paper store oohing and aahing over a really nice handmade/hand-dyed sheet of rice paper. But no matter the source, the outcome is the same: one of fleeting satisfaction because I had an idea for another project while working on that particular one. Paper crafting is an addiction that makes life a bit more shiny and bright.

Richela Fabian Morgan

Richela is the author of four published books: *Tape It & Make It* (Barron's Educational Series, 2012); *The Green Crafter, 52 Eco-Friendly Crafts for Every Week of the Year* (Citadel, 2009); *Noteworthy: Homemade Greeting Cards for Any Occasion*, a popular card-crafting kit (MetroBooks, 2008); and *Baby By the Numbers*, an essential reference guide to raising baby from birth to three years old (Chronicle, 2008). Ms. Morgan has her own website, **richelafabianmorgan.com**, on which she writes about making "stuff," teaching eco-crafts to friendly (and not so friendly) kids, and finding treasures on the streets of her village. She lives in Larchmont, New York, with her husband and two children.

Website: richelafabianmorgan.com

HOW TO MAKE THE TOTE BAG

STEP 1 Straighten out each of the 87 handles. The sum of handles is broken down into the following: 22 each for the front and back panels, 9 each for the left side, right side, and bottom, and 8 each for the two straps.

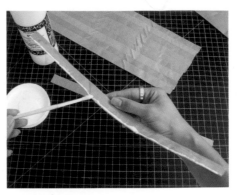

STEP 2 Create the front and back panels by layering the handles horizontally. The handles should overlap by ⅛ inch (3 mm). Apply glue at these edges with a small paintbrush. Allow at least 10 minutes for the glue to dry before proceeding to the next step.

STEP 3 To form the front and back panels, use the lines of the cutting mat as a guide. Keep the outer edges as straight as possible.

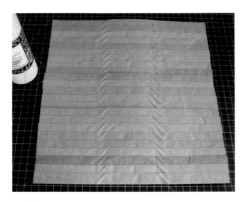

STEP 4 The front and back panels should be the same size and the edges should be straight.

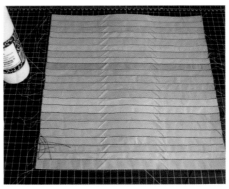

STEP 5 Use a sewing machine to sew the handle strips together using a straight stitch. An all-purpose needle should be sufficient. Be sure to clear the lower chamber containing the bobbin of any excess paper debris.

STEP 6 Double-knot the loose threads on the sides and trim excess with scissors, leaving no more than ⅛-inch (3 mm) tails.

STEP 7 Repeat steps 2 through 6 for the left/right sides and bottom. Be sure each section has 9 handles. Also be sure the width of the bottom panel is the same as the width of the front and back panels and that the length of the side panels matches the length of the front and back panels.

STEP 8 Working with the 9 handle bottom section and a pencil and ruler, measure and draw lines that are ⅛ inch (3 mm) from the outer left and right edges.

Tips!

Use binder clips to connect the front and back panels to the sides/bottom piece. The panels should be placed "wrong" (interior) sides together. While sewing each edge with the sewing machine, remove a few binder clips at a time. First use a straight stitch, then sew each edge again using a small zig-zag stitch as additional reinforcement.

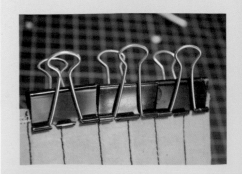

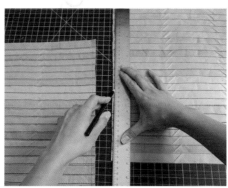

STEP 9 Sew the left and right sides to the bottom piece along the drawn lines. Flip over so the exterior side is facing down. Cover the interior side with duct tape, but be sure that at least a 1-inch (2.5 cm) border around the outer edges is left bare.

STEP 10 With the pencil and ruler, measure and draw two lines; each will be 1/8 inch (3 mm) from the outer left and right edges of the front panel. From these two lines, move 2 inches (5 cm) in toward the center. Draw another set of lines. Repeat on the back panel. This marks where the shoulder straps will be sewn.

STEP 11 For the bottom part of the shoulder straps, take 8 handles and pair them up. Glue each pair together by placing one handle on top of the other to double their strength. You will have 4 glued pieces. Allow at least ten minutes for the glue to dry.

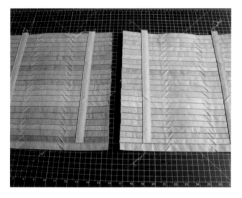

STEP 12 Using the interior lines drawn in step 10 as guidelines, sew the bottom parts of the shoulder straps to the front and back panels. Be sure the upper portions extend past the top edges of the panels by 1/8 inch (3 mm).

STEP 13 Flip over the front and back panels so the interior sides are facing up. Cover with duct tape, but be sure that at least a 1-inch (2.5 cm) border around the outer edges is left bare.

STEP 14 Repeat step 11, but be sure that the last inch (2.5 cm) of the paired ends is left unglued. Slip the unglued ends over the top edges of the front and back panels where the bottom parts of the shoulder straps extend. Add glue to the inside and press down. Secure with binder clips until the glue dries and the bottom and top parts of the shoulder straps are connected. Reinforce the connecting areas with decorative box stitching for added support.

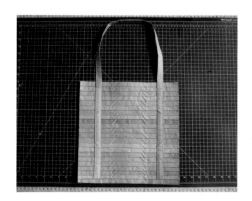

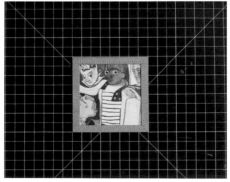

STEP 15 Sew the top parts of the shoulder straps together. They should overlap by 3 inches (7.6 cm). Not only do the straps provide an easy way to carry the tote bag, but they also serve to make it strong and durable by extending down the full length of the bag.

STEP 16 Add decorative flair to the bag front by cutting out a 4 x 4-inch (10 x 10 cm) image from a newspaper or magazine. Place the self-adhesive laminating sheet over it. Trim excess laminate with a craft knife and metal ruler. Trim the piece of cardboard down to 4 x 4 inches (10 x 10 cm).

STEP 17 Measure 1 inch inward from all four edges of the cardboard square and draw an inner 3 x 3-inch (7.6 x 7.6 cm) square. Carefully cut out the inside square to create a frame. Place the frame over the laminated image and sew together around all four sides. Glue to the front panel. Rub a little beeswax on the exterior of the bag.

CHAPTER 3

JEWELRY

Paper jewelry never fails to start a
conversation! Follow the steps to create
five unique necklaces.

JUNGLE BEADS NECKLACE

by Licia Politis

This necklace is one I created to go with a new outfit. The idea that flat paper can become a three-dimensional object excites me, and then for it to be functional is a bonus! The reaction of viewers is interesting when I tell them the beads are made from ordinary paper. These instructions are specific to my necklace, but keep in mind that yours will be just as unique if the bead sizes and colors are varied. The weight of the paper I used to make my beads was 120 gsm, but experiment with papers on hand to make beads of a pleasing size. Copy paper works well, as does lightweight cardstock. Cut the strips with the grain of the paper for smooth rolling.

Licia Politis

Licia has been creating art pieces with paper for over twenty years. She enjoys pushing the boundaries with such a humble medium, and has been awarded many accolades for her work, particularly in the art of quilling. Licia's creations have been exhibited in The Sydney Royal Easter Show from 1997 to 2012, The Museum of Brisbane in 2008, and the 2005 Art on Paper exhibition at Hazelhurst Regional Gallery. She was honored with a Fellowship Award of the English Quilling Guild in 2010. Her work has been featured in *Practical Quilling* (Anne Redman, Simon and Schuster AU, 2002) and *Australian Paper Crafts* magazine.

Why Paper?
Paper is probably the most accessible medium in today's world. I enjoy the challenge of working with it, and like the way paper can be transformed from a flat sheet into a 3D object.

SUPPLIES AND TOOLS

White paper 18 strips, 1 x 12 inches (2.5 x 30 cm)
White paper 4 strips, ½ x 12 inches (13 mm x 30 cm)
Black paper 3 strips, ½ x 1.5 inches (13 mm x 38 mm)
Decorative spacers silver (metal), 26
Fine cord silver, 36 inches (91 cm)
Eyelash yarn black, 40 inches (1 meter)
Paper trimmer
Ruler
Marker pen fine-tip black, permanent, waterproof
Black ink pad
PVA white glue
Quick-setting craft glue
Bamboo stick
Toothpicks
Corkboard
Large eye sewing needle
Matte spray varnish

HOW TO MAKE THE JUNGLE BEADS NECKLACE

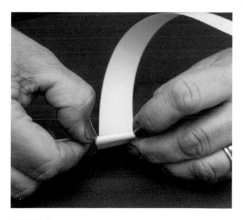

STEP 1 Make beads: Measure and cut 25 strips of paper as indicated in the Supplies and Tools list. Roll each strip on a bamboo stick.

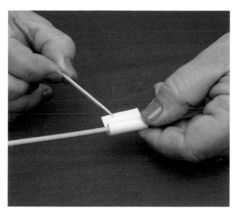

STEP 2 Glue the end with PVA glue.

The result will be these cylinders that will be our beads in making the necklace.

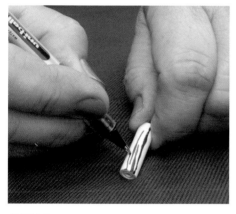

STEP 3 Hold a bead between the thumb and index finger and use a black marker to draw an animal print design. Turn the bead slowly until the whole bead is covered with the desired pattern. Repeat this step with all of the beads except for a few of the 1/2-inch (13 mm) beads.

STEP 4 While holding the shaft of a bead between thumb and index finger, press each end gently into the ink pad to blacken it. Allow the ink to dry completely.

STEP 5 Attach each jungle pattern bead to the corkboard with a toothpick. Spray matte varnish gently, covering all sides. Allow beads to dry and spray again with an extra coat of varnish.

STEP 6 Glue a strip of black paper around the remaining few 1/2-inch (13 mm) beads. Press covered black beads ends in ink pad or leave white.

Tips!

To determine paper grain, tear a sheet vertically and then horizontally. The tear with the grain will be quite straight, whereas the tear against the grain will be more jagged.

Make extra beads to experiment with hand drawn designs.

It might seem easier to draw on flat strips first and then roll them, but the design would not appear continuous when the strips are rolled.

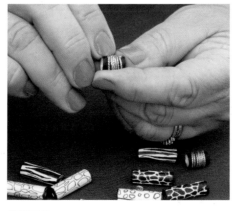

STEP 7 Apply a small amount of quick-setting craft glue to the end of the fine silver cord. Adhere the cord to one end of a 1/2-inch (13 mm) black bead and hold it in place until the glue sets. Wind the cord around the bead and glue the end in place. Repeat this step with the other black beads.

STEP 8 Thread the sewing needle with eyelash yarn and thread the beads onto the yarn, alternating paper and metal spacer beads. Allow the yarn to fray out between the beads.

STEP 9 Knot the yarn ends at the desired length so the necklace can be slipped on and off over your head.

INTRODUCTION TO QUILLING:
QUILLED PENDANTS
by Ann Martin

I first gave paper a twirl shortly after seeing a magazine article that featured intricate Valentines and monograms shaped from tiny paper coils and scrolls. Instantly captivated by the elegant look and seemingly magical things that could be done by rolling and pinching paper strips, I was determined to learn every aspect of quilling. I bought a few supplies and set to work, teaching myself via books and online instructions. Even when not quilling, I find myself making mental notes of design details I see around me. Perhaps a wrought iron gate, a flower arrangement,

or an antique ring of keys catches my eye and sparks a new project. I especially like that the process of quilling forces me to sit quietly, lost in my thoughts, while I create art from unlikely bits of paper.

There are so many ways to use quilling, it's limited only by one's imagination. Some quillers focus on incredibly small and intricately detailed three dimensional figures, while a few brave souls have ventured into large scale museum installations. One of my very favorite uses of the art is filigree jewelry. A quilled pendant can be made in an evening and worn the very next day.

As quilling requires so few supplies, chances are excellent that most people already have on hand what is needed to give it a try. Many arts and crafts stores sell packages of multi-color strips and a basic tool, and specialty papers and additional tools are available from online suppliers. However, if one is hesitant to buy supplies or just can't wait to get started, it's easy to cut practice strips by running a sheet of copy paper or junk mail through a shredder. A cake tester from the kitchen drawer, quilting needle, or even a round toothpick can serve as a substitute tool. Lastly, one requirement that isn't available for purchase is a fair amount of patience. With a little practice, however, coils will soon be evenly sized and smoothly rolled. I can almost predict a person will find the timeless art of quilling to be a relaxing and satisfying hobby.

TEARDROP ORB PENDANT

No one would believe at first glance that this pendant is made of paper! Not only is it lightweight and comfortable to wear, but it's also surprisingly sturdy. The design is composed of teardrop coils, domed tight coils, marquise ring coils, and a ring coil. Before making the individual shapes, however, one must learn to roll quilling strips smoothly and to pinch them into various shapes.

General Quilling Tips!

Because this project involves a pair of quilled coils that should appear as similar to one another as possible, the paper must be rolled smoothly. There's no way around it, this work requires even finger tension and practice. A little trick: use a straight pin to "jiggle" the inner coils and space them evenly after a coil is rolled, but before it is pinched and glued.

Use a damp cloth to keep fingers free of glue and to gently wipe stray glue bits from rolled coils before the glue has a chance to dry completely. No glue should show on a finished project.

Use a plastic lid as a glue palette. Squeeze a small amount of glue onto the lid and use a pin or the tip of a paper piercing tool to dip from the puddle. This works well to control the amount, less is more!

I've never found it necessary to apply a fixative to quilled pendants because necklaces are usually handled very little when worn. A matte finish fixative may be applied by spraying or brushing it on, but it may cause the coil centers to expand. Experiment with spare coils first.

SUPPLIES AND TOOLS

Quilling paper silver-edge black, ⅛ inch (3 mm), 1 package (jjquilling.co.uk or whimsiquills.com)
Quilling paper black, ⅛ inch (3 mm) 1 package
Quilling tool needle or slotted (the ultra-fine slotted tool I use is available from Japanese online shop, e-bison.ocnk.net)
Paper piercing tool to roll ring coil
Dowel or wood handle quilling tool—approximately ½ inch (13 mm) diameter to roll marquise ring coils
Scissors
Ruler
Tweezers
Glue dries clear, suitable for paper (Martha Stewart Crafts - All-Purpose Gel Adhesive)
Ball head pins
Plastic lid as glue palette
Damp cloth
Non-stick work surface acrylic sheet or Styrofoam tray
Jump ring silver, ¼ inch (6 mm)
Flat nose jewelry pliers 2 pairs
Silver necklace

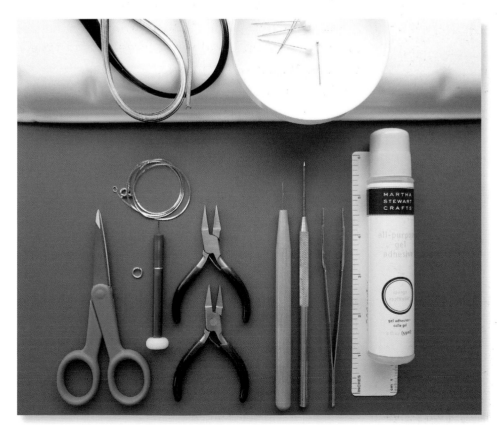

Tip!
Quilling paper is available in single or mixed color packages usually containing 30-100 strips.

HOW TO MAKE THE COILS

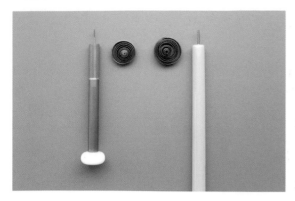

STEP 1 **Choosing a tool:** The decision of which type of quilling tool to use, slotted or needle, is best left up to the individual. A standard slotted tool is extremely easy to use, but the slot generally produces an obvious crimp in the center of the coil. Ultra-fine slotted tools are more widely available than they were just a few years ago, and they offer the advantage of producing a very tiny crimp.

STEP 2 Another option is a needle tool. It can be a bit tricky to master and may lead to hand fatigue more quickly than using a slotted tool, but the end result is a coil with a perfectly round, small center.

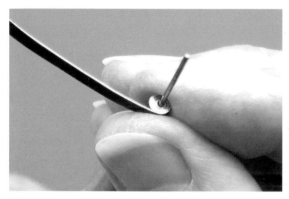

STEP 3 **To roll a coil with a needle tool:** Dampen fingertips and curve one end of a paper strip across the needle. Roll the strip around the needle with the thumb and index finger of whichever hand feels most comfortable, while holding the tool handle with the other hand. Apply firm, even pressure while taking care to roll the paper, not the tool.

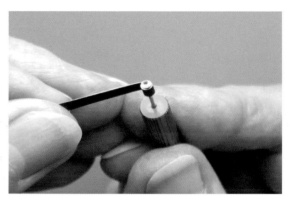

STEP 4 **To roll a coil with a slotted tool:** Slide the end of a strip just into the slot, but not beyond it. Turn the tool with one hand while evenly guiding the strip with the other.

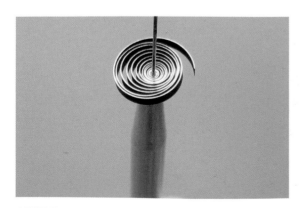

STEP 5 Whether using a needle tool or slotted tool, when the strip is fully rolled, allow the coil to relax and slide it off the tool.

STEP 6 This relaxed coil is called a loose coil. The end may be glued in place or left unglued until after the coil is pinched to make a different shape.

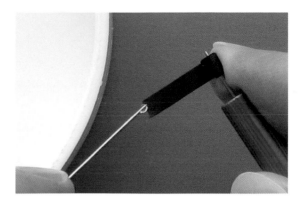

STEP 7 Tight coil: Glue the torn end in place while the coil is still rolled on the tool.

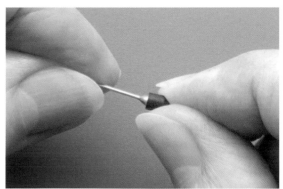

STEP 8 Domed tight coil: Press gently against one flat side of tight coil with the rounded head of a pin.

Tips!

A torn end blends best on a circular loose or tight coil so it will look perfectly smooth and round.

When making shapes such as a teardrop or marquise, pinch the loose coil near the strip end, glue the end, and trim excess paper.

STEP 9 Apply a coating of glue inside the dome to maintain the curved shape.

STEP 10 Teardrop: Make a relaxed coil. Slip it off the tool. Adjust inner coils evenly with a pin.

STEP 11 Pinch to create a point.

Example teardrop

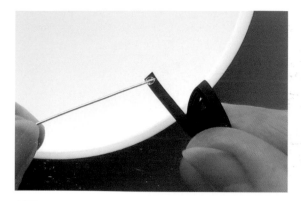

STEP 12 Glue end and trim the excess paper.

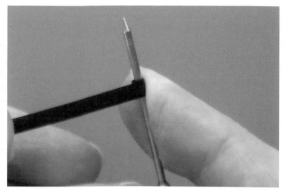

STEP 13 Ring coil: Wrap a 3-inch (7.6 cm) strip (approximate) around the tip of a paper piercing tool six times and glue the torn end in place. The resulting coil center must be large enough to accommodate a jump ring.

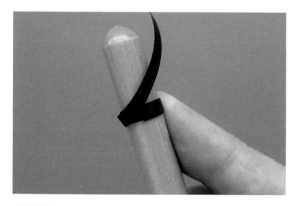

STEP 14 Marquise ring coil: Roll a 9-inch (23 cm) strip (approximate) around a 1/2-inch (13 mm) dowel or needle tool handle seven times.

STEP 15 Slide coil off tool and gently pull the end of the strip to make a snug circle. Pinch two opposing points to create a marquise ring coil. Glue end and trim excess paper.

HOW TO ASSEMBLE THE TEARDROP ORB PENDANT

STEP 1 Components:
- 17-inch (43 cm) silver-edge black teardrop (make 2)
- 9-inch (23 cm) black marquise ring coil (make 4)
- 2 1/2-inch (6.5 cm) silver-edge black domed tight coil (make 1)
- 2 1/2-inch (6.5 cm) black domed tight coil (make 6)
- 2-inch (5 cm) silver-edge black domed tight coil (make 2)
- 3-inch (7.6 cm) black ring coil (make 1)

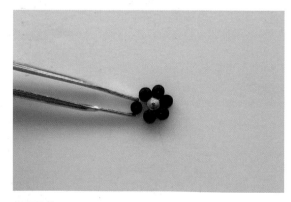

STEP 2 Assemble the six 2 1/2-inch (6.5 cm) black domed tight coils around the 2 1/2-inch (6.5 cm) silver-edge black domed tight coil to make the flower.

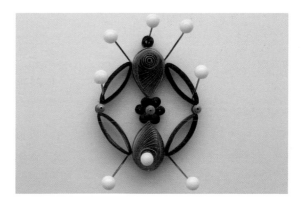

STEP 3 Assemble all remaining components and hold in place with pins on the non-stick work surface while the glue dries: **A.** Glue a teardrop above and below the flower. **B.** Arrange two marquise ring coils on each side of teardrops with a 2-inch (5 cm) silver-edge black tight coil placed between each marquise ring coil. **C.** Glue the black ring coil to the curve of the top teardrop.

STEP 4 After the glue has dried, reinforce pendant strength by turning the pendant over and dotting glue on the join spots. Allow glue to dry completely overnight.

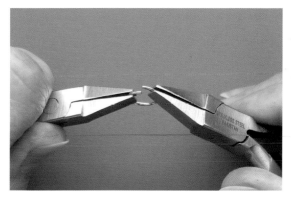

STEP 5 Open the jump ring and slip it through the black ring coil. Close the ring.

Tip!

To easily open and close a jump ring, the split should be positioned at the top. Grasp each side of the split with flat nose jewelry pliers. With a gentle twisting motion, move one side away from the body while the other side is held steady. Reverse the process to smoothly close the jump ring.

STEP 6 Thread a necklace chain through the jump ring. Wear and enjoy!

SUPPLIES AND TOOLS

Quilling paper gold-edge black, ⅛ inch (3 mm),
  1 package (jjquilling.co.uk or whimsiquills.com)
Metallic paper antique gold, light to medium weight
Quilling tool needle or slotted (the ultra-fine slotted
  tool I use is available from Japanese online shop,
  e-bison.ocnk.net)
Stiff wire
Dowel approximately ½ inch (13 mm) diameter
  (ZIG marker or wood handle quilling tool)
Scissors
Ruler
Tweezers
Glue dries clear, suitable for paper (Martha Stewart
  Crafts - All-Purpose Gel Adhesive)
Ball head pins to shape domed coils, apply glue, and
  position coils while drying
Plastic lid as glue palette
Damp cloth to keep fingers free of glue
Non-stick work surface
Jump ring gold, ¼ inch (6 mm)
Flat nose jewelry pliers 2 pairs
Gold necklace
Paper trimmer to cut rectangle from metallic paper
  (optional)
Paper piercing tool to apply glue (optional)

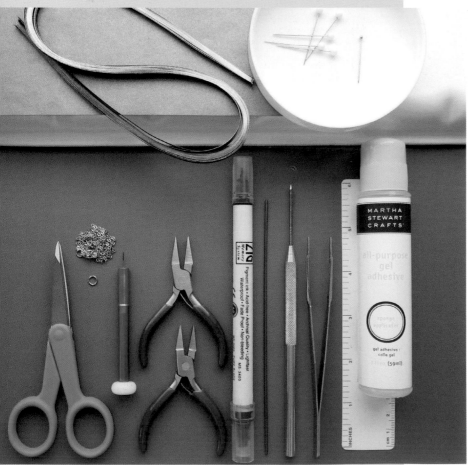

ANTIQUE KEY PENDANT

by Ann Martin

Perhaps your eye has been caught by the trend of antique keys worn as jewelry. Now you can make your very own version that looks as convincing as an honest-to-goodness key! It's so very comfortable to wear too—no neck ache from the pull of heavy metal. After all, few materials are lighter than bits of rolled paper.

I was inspired to quill this design after noticing an ornate key in the lock of an old Victrola that had been hidden away in the attic of a Pennsylvania farmhouse. Be on the lookout for a variety of decorative keys and try your hand at making them too. Once coil rolling has been mastered, there will be no stopping you from creating more designs.

Ann Martin

Editor and designer Ann Martin's paper quilling has been featured widely across all media. Via her popular blog, *All Things Paper*, she features quilling tutorials and introduces a variety of paper artisans, many of whom have created the projects in this book. Ann appeared on the HGTV television show *That's Clever* to demonstrate quilling, and her designs have been published in *Quill It Easy* and *1000 Handmade Greetings – Creative Cards and Clever Correspondence*. She is a frequent contributor to paper craft magazines and craft websites. Ann's quilling was shown in a solo exhibit at the Brandywine River Museum in Chadds Ford, Pennsylvania. She enjoys teaching others to quill, and creates custom quilled marriage certificates, ketubot, and wedding invitations.

Website: allthingspaper.net

Why Paper?
Paper fascinates me. It can take on a myriad of shapes, is often forgiving, and its very being inspires creativity. The wide array of colors and textures make it aesthetically appealing, and the low cost of paper gives a certain freedom to stretch my imagination, play with it, and try new things.

Working with paper suits my personality because I find great satisfaction as a quilled piece slowly takes shape under my fingers. I appreciate neatness just as much as beauty, and love that the end result is the complete opposite of the tangled pile of strips that litter my desk as I begin a project.

I think people feel connected to paper because it is such a natural part of everyday life. Thus, they appreciate the element of surprise it has the potential of producing... things can be made with paper that most would never expect or imagine!

HOW TO MAKE THE ANTIQUE KEY PENDANT

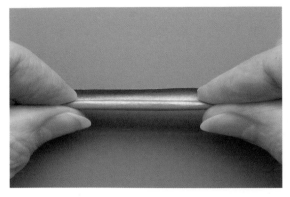

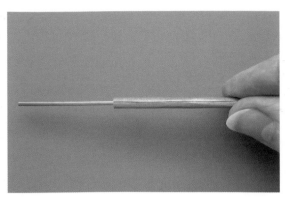

Tip!
Before rolling the rectangle on the wire, soften the fibers of the paper by rolling it in both directions around the handle of a quilling tool a few times.

STEP 1a Cut a ³/₄ x 1⁵/₈-inch (19 mm x 4 cm) rectangle of metallic gold paper with scissors or a paper trimmer. Roll the rectangle lengthwise around a stiff wire or if you have a cake tester in your kitchen drawer, it will work well too.

STEP 1b Apply a small amount of glue with a pin or paper piercing tool along the rolled edge, and slide the tube off the wire. Hold the rolled edge with a light touch for a few minutes while the glue sets. Wipe away excess glue with a damp cloth. Set aside to dry completely.

STEP 2 Make the teeth of the key: Cut a strip of metallic gold paper that measures approximately ¹/₄ x 3 inches (6 mm x 7.6 cm), and another that measures ¹/₈ x 2 inches (3 mm x 5 cm). Roll strip on tool, allow it to relax, slide it off the tool, and pinch the coil at two opposing points to make a **marquise coil**. Glue the end and trim excess paper.

STEP 3 Working on a non-stick surface, assemble the key shaft: Position the seamed edge so that it is the center back of the shaft. Glue the larger tooth on the lower right side of the shaft approximately ¹/₈ inch (3 mm) from the bottom. Glue the smaller tooth above it, leaving a small space between the two.

STEP 4 Make the two metallic gold marquise coils that will be located at the top of the key shaft: Cut a strip of paper that measures ¹/₈ x 2¹/₂ inches (3 mm x 6.5 cm) and another that is slightly less than ¹/₈ x 3 inches (3 mm x 7.6 cm). Roll each strip as in Step 2, center and glue the narrower coil at the top of the key shaft. Position and glue the wider marquise directly above it.

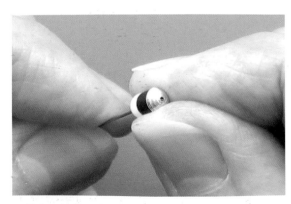

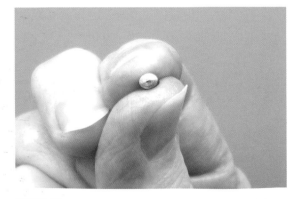

STEP 5a Cut a 4-inch (10 cm) strip of gold-edge black quilling paper and tear one end. Roll the strip beginning with the cut end. Without allowing the coiled paper to relax, glue the torn end in place. Slip this tight coil off the tool. Use a pin to gently press against one side of the tight coil to curve it.

STEP 5b Pinch the coil gently between thumb and index finger to shape it into an oval. **STEP 5c** Apply a small amount of glue inside the dome to preserve the shape. **STEP 5d** Glue this **domed oval tight coil** horizontally at the top of the key shaft directly above the two marquises.

STEP 6 Make the large marquise ring coil: Snugly wrap gold-edge black quilling paper six times around a dowel (I used a ZIG marker) that measures approximately ½ inch (13 mm) in diameter.

STEP 7 Slide the coil off the dowel without allowing it to relax, pinch two opposing points, glue the end in place, and trim excess paper. Glue one pointed end of the marquise to the domed tight coil at the top of the key shaft.

STEP 8 Make the gold-edge black quilled coils that surround the large ring coil marquise:

- Four 2½-inch (6.5 cm) domed oval tight coil
- Two 2½-inch (6.5 cm) marquise
- Two 4-inch (10 cm) teardrop
- Two 6-inch (15 cm) marquise
- Two 6-inch (15 cm) teardrop
- Two 7-inch (18 cm) marquise
- Two 7-inch (18 cm) teardrop

To make a teardrop coil: Roll a strip on the quilling tool. Allow the coil to expand, slip it off the tool, and pinch the coil close to the end of the strip. Glue end in place and trim excess paper.

Tip!
Notice that the coil pairs are mirror images of one another; in other words, note the rotation of the inner coils. This is accomplished by rolling the paper strip positioned with the metallic edge on top for one coil, and with the metallic edge pointing downward for the mirror image coil.

STEP 9 Referring to photo of the key pinned on the work board: **A.** Glue a 7-inch (18 cm) teardrop horizontally on each side of the oval domed tight coil at the top of the key shaft with points facing outward. **B.** Working upwards along each side of the large ring coil marquise, glue the pairs of 7-inch (18 cm) marquises, 6-inch (15 cm) teardrops, and 6-inch (15 cm) marquises in place, each coil angled upward with points facing outward.

C. Glue the 4-inch (10 cm) teardrops, 2½-inch (6.5 cm) marquises, and 2½-inch (6.5 cm) domed oval tight coils in place, lodging them between the larger teardrops and marquises. **STEP 10** Turn the key over and apply small dots of glue as reinforcement on all joined areas. Allow the key to dry completely before handling. Overnight is best.

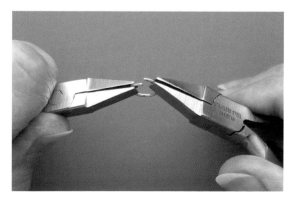

STEP 11 Open the jump ring and insert it through the top point of the large marquise ring coil. Close the jump ring and thread a necklace chain through it. Wear and enjoy!

FINE PAPER YARN NECKLACE

by **Linda Thalmann**

Seven strands of beaded chain stitches join together to create an organically shaped, crocheted choker. Part of its charm is the irregularity of the small loops. Work only with your fingers to achieve this effect—there's no need for a crochet hook!

Linda Thalmann

With a lifelong passion for paper and MA degrees in Textile/Art & Design (Kunstuniversität, Linz, Austria) and in Art History (Paris-Lodron University, Salzburg, Austria), Linda Thalmann dedicates her time and artistic talent to paper yarns and paper twines. She has exhibited in the whole of Europe, given lectures on weaving and paper textiles, and was featured in *Paper Textiles* (Christina Leitner, Haupt, Germany, 2005, A&C Black, England, 2005) as one of the youngest contributors. She founded *PaperPhine* in 2009 to make the nearly forgotten paper yarns and paper twines available again to a broad audience, and has published her ideas and insights on **paperphine.com** ever since.

> ## Why Paper?
> I can't think of a time when paper was not an important part of my life. My mum says the best way to keep me quiet as a small child was to give me paper and pens. By the age of ten I was already boasting about my paper collection, and two years later I had my very own papermaking workshop in my parents' backyard. I'm forever grateful to them for their support in my early artistic and sometimes quite messy endeavours!
>
> When the time came to decide what to do with my life—or at least in which courses the next couple of years would be best spent—I chose the art school's textile and fiber department because they also had paper making facilities. This is where I not only discovered a lot of textile techniques to incorporate into my work, but also fine paper yarns and paper twines that were the ideal material to use. I was able to combine my passion for paper with my newly learned textile skills.
>
> The paper yarn necklace presented in this book combines an old and basic textile technique with the unique characteristics of paper and paper yarns. Without the paper yarn's stiffness and lightness—or what I like to call the paper yarn's own will—as well as its smooth texture and elegant look, making this necklace would not have been possible.

Tips!
Finest paper yarn is fairly easy to work with once the fingers have become used to it. It might feel slightly slippery in the beginning, but work with a light touch. There is no need to pull on the yarn with force.

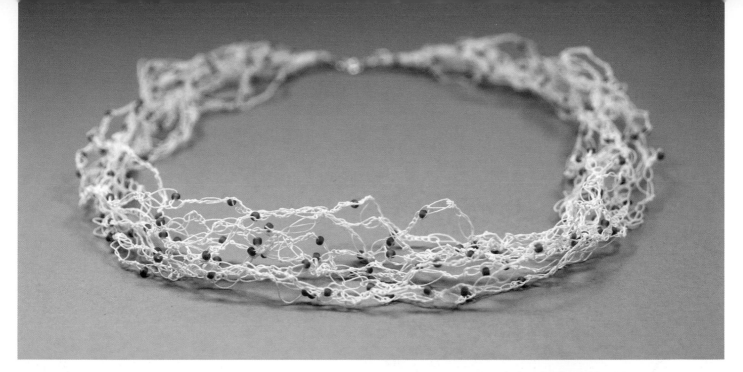

SUPPLIES AND TOOLS

Finest paper yarn about 30 yards (28 meters)
(paperphine.com)
Seed beads 200, size 11 or 12 is ideal, but beads
can also be smaller or larger. For the necklace as shown,
size 11 beads in a reddish hue and a matte finish were
used, but of course any favorite beads and colors
can be substituted
Jump rings 2
Spring ring with matching clasp counterpart—a toggle clasp
or a clasp style of your choice may be used to finish the
paper yarn necklace
Transparent glue
Paper clips 2
Scissors

HOW TO MAKE THE PAPER YARN NECKLACE

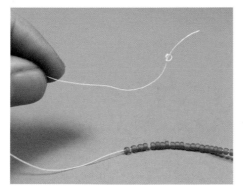

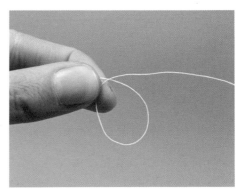

STEP 1 Thread 200 seed beads onto the paper yarn. Paper yarn is quite stiff, so there isn't a need to use a needle. Move the beads away from the end of the yarn and toward the spool. Continue doing this while working to prevent too many beads from slipping toward the crocheting area at once and onto the crocheted strands.

STEP 2 After the beads have been threaded, make a knot at the end of the paper yarn that is big enough so the beads can't slip over it.

STEP 3 To start crocheting, leave about 8 inches (20 cm) of paper yarn from the knot and hold this end with the left index finger and thumb. Grasp the yarn with the fingers of the right hand and create a loop. The paper yarn spool and the threaded beads are both off to the right side at this point.

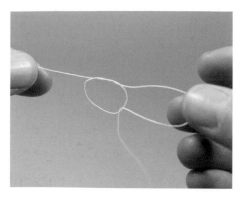

STEP 4 Carefully put two fingers through the loop from the front and pull the working yarn through the loop to make the the first chain stitch.

STEP 5 Slowly pull this first chain stitch to tighten the starting loop.

Tip!
To better control the working yarn it helps to wind it twice around the index finger of the left hand.

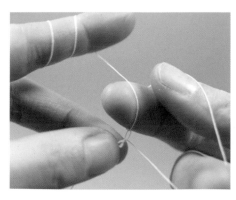

STEP 6 All of the following chain stitches are worked just like the first one—pull the working yarn through the last loop to create each new loop. The loops should not be pulled completely tight; allow a diameter of about 0.1-0.2 inches (2.5-5 mm) to remain open for a lacy effect.

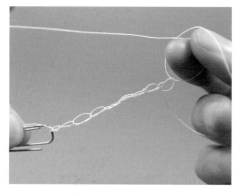

STEP 7 After crocheting the first 2 inches (5 cm), slightly open one paper clip and put it into the first loop of the necklace. The paper clip helps keep track of the number of strands that will be made (a total of seven) and will keep them an equal length.

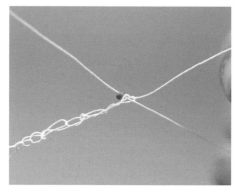

STEP 8 To add the first bead, let one bead slip towards the working area and continue to crochet. The bead will automatically become part of the working loop and then be incorporated into the crocheted strand.

STEP 9 The first bead is firmly in place.

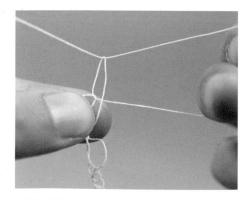

STEP 10 Sometimes it can be tricky to prevent pulling the loops too tightly. To keep them quite loose and large, hold the last, still large loop between the thumb and index finger while making and tightening the next one.

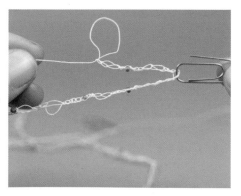

STEP 11 Once the first strand has reached the desired necklace length, add the second paper clip to the last chain stitch to mark this length. 22-24 inches (56-61 cm) is good for a medium length necklace, but also check the length in front of a mirror to see what looks best. Now turn the work and make chain stitches back along this length to create another strand.

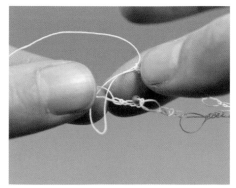

STEP 12a Beginning with the second strand, the single strands should be joined every 4-6 inches (10-15 cm). To do this, carefully put the working loop through one of the big loops of another strand and continue crocheting. It doesn't matter which strands are joined—actually it's best to mix things up and join different ones rather than just the previously completed strand. This way the necklace will still be quite loose without looking twisted.

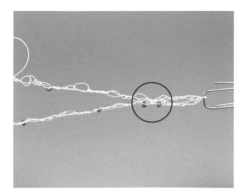

STEP 12b Now two strands have been joined together. **STEP** 13a Whenever a paper clip is reached, indicating the end of that row, slip the last chain stitch onto the paper clip. Turn the work and continue crocheting until seven strands have been completed.

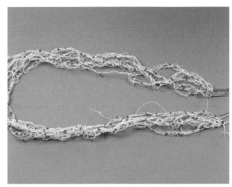

STEP 13b Once the seventh strand is finished, leave an additional 8 inches (20 cm) of paper yarn and cut it. Pull the loose end of the yarn through the working loop, tighten it to fasten off, and put this end onto the paper clip as well.

STEP 14a Add a latch to finish the necklace: Open a jump ring and thread it through the same loops as one of the paper clips. Add either the spring ring or its counterpart (or whatever clasp was chosen) to the jump ring as well, and close the jump ring securely.

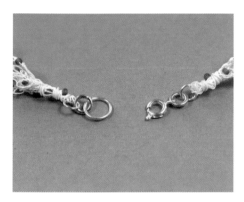

STEP 14b Remove the paperclip and repeat the process at the other end of the necklace.

STEP 15 Tightly wind the free length of paper yarn around the last 0.4 inch (10 mm) of the necklace and knot it. Repeat on the other end of the necklace.

Tips!

It is possible to open and close a jump ring with just the fingers, but using two flat or chain nose jewelry pliers makes it easier. Grasp each side of the jump ring opening with a pair of pliers, and move one side away from the body while the other side is held steady. Reverse the process to smoothly close the jump ring.

STEP 16 To prevent the wound paper yarn from slipping and the knot from opening, use two or three drops of transparent glue on each end of the necklace. This will also give additional strength to the ends as they are the parts that will be handled most often.

Tips!

To preserve the necklace, avoid contact with water. Paper yarn can get wet, but then it will tear more easily.

To retain the shape of the necklace, use care while handling. Relax in the knowledge that paper yarn regains its strength once it dries.

STEP 17 Ready to wear!!

LOOSELY BRAIDED MAKIGAMI PENDANT

by Benjamin John Coleman

I first began experimenting with tightly rolled newspaper in 2009. At the time I was making sculptures from twigs I harvested from the local woods. I'd mount the twig to a rock and then attach leaves and flowers that I folded from paper. I called these sculptures *Origami Bonsai*, which is also the title of my first book on the subject, published by Tuttle Publishing in April of 2010. This arrangement worked well, but I recognized an issue that could turn into a problem. The grove of Mountain Laurel bushes from which I cut my twigs was showing signs of overharvesting. I had collected most of the branches that grew in impressive and unexpected ways, and it was taking more time to find twigs suitable for Origami Bonsai sculptures.

So I wanted to make twigs from paper, and thought about things I had been exposed to that were similar. I soon realized that lollipop sticks are made from paper and began working with photocopy paper. I tried rolling it tightly, but it tended to unroll. Then I tried saturating it with water, and then a mixture of water and paint, and then rolling it. I soon discovered I was running out of photocopy paper and turned to the only other paper I had at the time, the morning's newspaper.

As soon as I saturated the paper I knew I was onto something. It behaved differently. It didn't collapse and twist. Instead, the paper tended to slide over itself as I gently rolled it, slowly tightening, and becoming a solid strip of paper. I put it into my car, parked in the hot sun, to cure. A few hours later I had an amazingly light, yet strong strip of paper. I then discovered methods for creating tapered strips, and made intricate, natural looking twig assemblies.

I call the material, and the technique for making it, makigami. *Maki* means roll in Japanese, and *gami* means paper. We'll be using five makigami strips, and the ancient art of braiding, to make a beautiful, durable pendant from paper.

Benjamin John Coleman

Ben is the author of *Origami Bonsai* (Tuttle, 2010) and *Origami 101: Master Basic Skills and Techniques Easily through Step-by-Step Instruction* (Creative Publishing International, 2011).

Websites: origamibonsai.org and benagami.com

Why Paper?
When I realized that using twigs and wood for my origami bonsai sculptures was not sustainable, I turned to paper and found a wonderful medium that recycled my newspaper.

Visit tuttlepublishing.com to view a video in which Benjamin demonstrates the process of making and braiding the makigami pendant.

HOW TO MAKE MAKIGAMI ROLLING SOLUTION

I developed this recipe for makigami rolling solution with guidance from my cousin Gretchen Anderson, a curator with the Carnegie Museum of Natural History and an expert in glues and paper. At the time we wanted to make chopsticks from recycled paper and discovered that our sticks failed whenever lifting something heavy. Adding cornstarch to the solution solved the problem. I use this recipe whenever I'm making something that will be touched, worn, or handled frequently.

SUPPLIES AND TOOLS

Shallow cookie sheets 2 (You don't need to dedicate two cookie sheets to making makigami. As long as you wash the cookie sheets carefully they can be used to make cookies again.)
Paintbrush 1 inch (25 mm), flat
Paintbrush small and round
Latex gloves
Wide binder clip
Clamp or small vise to secure the binder clip
Clothespins
Newspaper
Scissors
Wax paper
Wire cutters or heavy duty nail cutters
Emery board
Paper towels
Shallow pan
Heat source
Craft knife
Drill bit 1/8 inch (3 mm)
Masking tape
Acrylic paint yellow, green

Durable Makigami Rolling Solution Recipe			
	Ratio	US	Metric
Water	32	2 cups	470 ml
Acrylic Paint (white)	2	2 tablespoons	30 ml
Wood Glue	2	2 tablespoons	30 ml
Corn Starch	1	1 tablespoon	15 ml

Combine the ingredients in a jelly jar and mix thoroughly. This will give you enough solution to make many pendants. The solution can be stored indefinitely.

HOW TO MAKE THE LOOSELY BRAIDED MAKIGAMI PENDANT

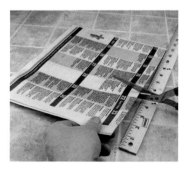

STEP 1 Gather a section of newspaper together. At least five pages will be needed because we're going to make a pendant with five strips. I urge you to make at least 10 strips, perhaps more, for practice.

STEP 2 Cut about 10 inches (25 cm) off the bottom of the section, cutting parallel to the fold.

STEP 3 Now cut about 4½ inches (11 cm) off the piece that was just made, but this time, cutting perpendicular to the fold.

STEP 4 Fold the area that was just cut in half widthwise. If unsure which direction to fold it, look at the blue stripe printed on the newspaper in these pictures. Compare the stripe to your newspaper.

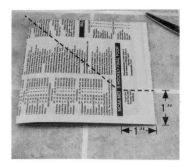

STEP 5 Cut all five sheets at once, starting 1 inch (2.5 cm) from the bottom edge, make a cut parallel to it that is 1 inch (2.5 cm) long. Then cut up at an angle to the top as shown.

STEP 6 After cutting, the paper should look like this. We're going to use the pieces at the bottom. Unfold them.

STEP 7 There should be five identical pieces of newspaper that look similar to this.

STEP 8 Gather two shallow cookie sheets, latex gloves, makigami rolling solution, a wide binder clip, a flat paintbrush, and clothespins. It's also a good idea to put on an apron. Wet a paper towel and put it on one of the cookie sheets.

STEP 9 Paint a layer of makigami rolling solution onto the second cookie sheet. The solution should cover about the same size area as the pieces of paper.

STEP 10 Put one of the pieces of newspaper into the pan and saturate it with rolling solution.

STEP 11 Insert the paintbrush bristles underneath the corner of the newspaper to lift and then flip it.

STEP 12 Run the brush over the entire surface to ensure it has been completely saturated. If necessary, add more rolling solution. Use the brush to remove any trapped air bubbles.

STEP 13 Use the brush's bristles to lift the leading edge, and then fold about ½ inch (13 mm) up.

STEP 14 Use the brush to remove any air bubbles under the fold.

STEP 15 Use the bristles to lift the folded leading edge, and curl it to form a tube.

STEP 16 Carefully roll the remaining paper onto the tube.

STEP 17 The tube should look like this. Lift it and...

STEP 18 ...gently roll it again.

STEP 19 Repeat steps 17 and 18 until the tube becomes a solid shaft of paper.

STEP 20 Knead the entire length of the strip by pinching it with both hands about 1/4 inch (6 mm) apart and then squeezing hands together. Knead the strip a second time.

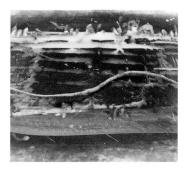

STEP 21 The kneaded strip should look like this.

STEP 22 Roll it a couple more times to remove any indentations left over from kneading.

STEP 23 Put the finished strip on top of a damp paper towel.

STEP 23a It's always a good idea to have extra pieces of newspaper ready in case of troublesome strip rolling.

STEP 24 Roll four more strips.

STEP 25 Align the ends of the strips.

STEP 26 Insert about 1/4 inch (6 mm) of the strips into a binder clip that has been secured so it won't move.

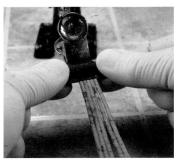

STEP 27 Squeeze the binder clip closed to ensure that none of the strips will fall out.

STEP 27a Use any type of paper clamp to hold the makigami strips while braiding. In this example, I've clamped a different type of paper clip to a cutting board.

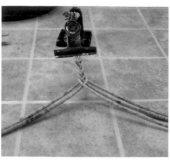

STEP 28 Begin loosely braiding, leaving an even gap between the strips. (Refer to the five strand braiding diagram below.)

STEP 29 Braid the entire length of the strips.

STEP 30 Gather the ends together.

HOW TO DO FIVE STRAND BRAIDING

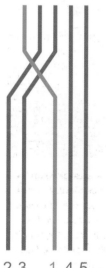

2 3   1 4 5

2 3 5   1 4

3 5   2 1 4

3 5 4   2 1

5 4   3 2 1

STEP 31 Insert them into a clothespin.

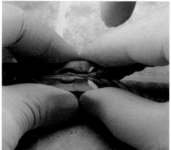

STEP 32 Squeeze the clothespin closed.

STEP 33 Shape the pendant into a teardrop shape.

STEP 34 Put the pendant in a pan.

STEP 35 And then put the pan in a car parked in the sun for about two hours.

STEP 36 Confirm that the pendant has cured completely by feel. It should be very hard and unwilling to bend. It should also feel extremely lightweight, and its color should appear slightly bleached.

STEP 37 Trim any loose paper with a craft knife.

STEP 38 Paint the area compressed by the clothespin with wood glue. Work the wood glue into all nooks and crannies and allow it to dry for at least one hour. Do not paint the entire pendant with wood glue in this step!

STEP 39 Use a 1/8-inch (3 mm) drill bit to bore a hole by hand through the wood glue reinforced area. I wrapped some masking tape on my drill bit to give me more leverage.

STEP 40 Use wire cutters or heavy duty nail clippers to cut off the excess makigami.

STEP 41 Use an emery board to remove any excess flakes of makigami.

STEP 42 Put a latex glove on the hand holding the pendant. Also put a sheet of wax paper over the work surface. Paint the pendant with a mixture of equal parts water, acrylic paint (I used yellow), and wood glue using the round paintbrush.

STEP 43 Set the pendant down on the wax paper and carefully inspect it. Make sure the paint has been worked into all the nooks and crannies, while at the same time has not been allowed to pool.

STEP 44 Once the first coat of paint has dried, paint a second coat of one part acrylic paint (I used green), one part wood glue, and 4 parts water.

STEP 45 The completed pendant should look similar to this. Try using different colors for the first and second coat to achieve different effects.

STEP 46 I call the finish on this pendant a composite because I used two different colors in the mixtures for the first and second coats.

MAKIGAMI PENDANT FLOWER

by Ann Martin

To adorn Ben's striking makigami pendant, I created this metallic paper flower with the aid of a cherry blossom punch. There's no need to be limited to just one specific punch for making flowers, however. Cut apart a variety of punched shapes and fold, bend, and position the segments in different ways. Chances are good you'll soon be creating a garden of dimensional blossoms!

SUPPLIES AND TOOLS

Sakura (cherry blossom) punch, 1¼ inch (32 mm) (CARL CarlaCraft)

Quilling paper gold-edge black, fern green, ⅛ inch (3 mm), (jjquilling.co.uk or whimsiquills.com)

Metallic paper green-gold, heavy paper or lightweight cardstock

Quilling tool needle or slotted (the ultra-fine slotted tool I use is available from Japanese online shop, e-bison.ocnk. net)

Scissors detail

Ruler

Tweezers

Glue strong, dries clear (Crafter's Pick: The Ultimate!)

Paper piercing tool or pin to apply glue

Plastic lid as glue palette

Damp cloth to keep fingers free of glue

Non-stick work surface

Jump ring gold 2 (5 mm, 8 mm)

Flat nose jewelry pliers 2 pairs

Gold necklace

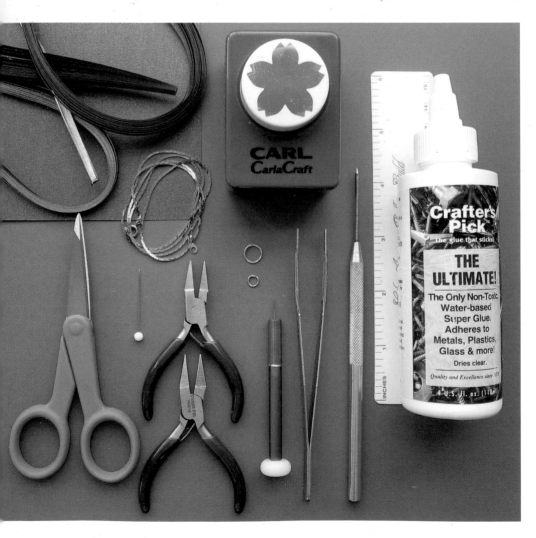

Tips!

Use a damp cloth to keep fingers free of glue and to gently wipe stray glue bits from rolled coils before the glue has a chance to dry completely.

Use a plastic lid as a glue palette. Squeeze a small amount of glue onto the lid and use a pin or the tip of a paper piercing tool to dip from the puddle. This works well to control the amount... less is more when it comes to gluing quilling!

HOW TO MAKE THE MAKIGAMI PENDANT FLOWER

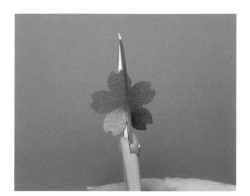

***STEP* 1** Punch three or four sakura blossoms from metallic paper. Carefully cut them apart to create a total of 15 individual petals of equal size and shape.

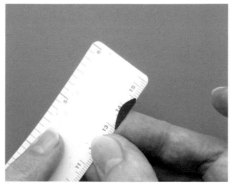

***STEP* 2** Fold each petal in half lengthwise using the edge of a ruler as a midline guide.

***STEP* 3** Working on a non-stick surface, apply a small amount of glue with a paper piercing tool or pin to each petal point (the unnotched end), joining them in a snug circle. Add one or two petals at a time and allow the glue to set for a few moments before adding another. When the circle is complete and nicely shaped, set it aside to dry completely.

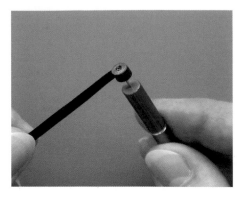

STEP 4a Measure and cut an 11-inch (28 cm) strip of gold-edge black quilling paper. Tear one end and insert the cut end into the quilling tool slot. Roll the entire strip.

STEP 4b Allow the coil to relax and slip it off the tool.

STEP 4c Hold the coil gently and pull the strip end. Wrap the loose paper tail around the coil by hand to create a thickened edge.

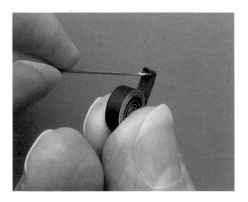

STEP 4d Glue end in place.

Example: loose coil with a thickened edge.

STEP 4e Glue the loose coil to the center of the petal circle.

Tip!
Spread a shallow puddle of glue on a plastic lid. Holding the coil with tweezers, touch its underside to the glue and place the coil directly on the flower.

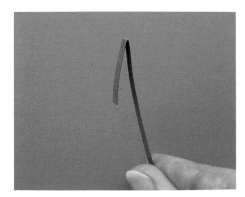

STEP 5a Make two "alternate side loop" fern green leaves. The small one is ⅝ inch (16 mm) in length and the large one is about 1⅛ inch (29 mm). Make a fold at one end of the strip. This is considered the first loop and will be the height of the finished leaf.

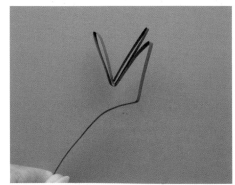

STEP 5b Continue using the same strip without cutting it. Make a loop to the left of the fold that isn't quite as tall as the first loop and then a matching loop to the right of the fold.

STEP 5c Make another pair of loops, slightly shorter than the first pair.

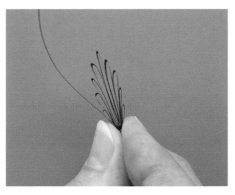

STEP 5d Continue making pairs of loops that descend in size: three pairs of loops for the 5/8-inch (16 mm) leaf and four or five pairs for the 1 1/8-inch (29 mm) leaf.

STEP 5e Encircle all of the loops with the same continuous strip to create a collar. Pinch the top to create a leaf tip.

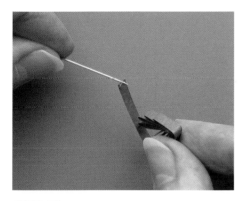

STEP 5f Glue and trim the end.

STEP 6 Position and glue the completed flower on the lower right side of the pendant with strong craft glue. Position and glue the two leaves on the underside of the flower petals, allowing the leaf tips to show.

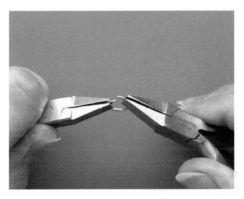

STEP 7 Open the large jump ring and insert it through the hole at the pendant top. Slip the small ring onto the large ring and close the large ring. Thread a necklace chain through the small jump ring.

Tip!
To easily open and close a jump ring, the split should be positioned at the top. Grasp each side of the split with flat nose jewelry pliers. With a gentle twisting motion, move one side away from the body while the other side is held steady. Reverse the process to smoothly close the jump ring.

Congratulations

CHAPTER 4

CORRESPONDENCE

Use a variety of paper crafting techniques to decorate a package with a clever dual-purpose gift tag, make cards for special occasions, and create a handmade travel journal.

FRAMEABLE TREE CARD

by Marnie B. Karger

Here's a fun paper cut project that can become an all-occasion greeting card or a decorative artwork worthy of framing. The project features a cheery little tree cut from the card, with a layer of colored paper set behind for a shadowed effect. Making the card employs multiple cutting techniques and requires some materials and tools that may add new skills to your crafting repertoire. While written to make a card, these directions will work for any size piece. See the variations section at the end for details.

Why Paper?

Paper is an amazingly accessible medium, and I've enjoyed working with it in a variety of ways. I really got into origami as a kid and filled my room with little folded paper friends. Later, my art instructor in high school taught me how to use an X-ACTO blade correctly, and since then I've been experimenting with different types of blades and cutting techniques. I first tried out a swivel blade right about the time the scrapbooking industry took off. All of these lovely, chromatically-related shades of cardstock were coming out, so it's as if a series of doors opened in front of me... I took my blade, walked through, and haven't really looked back. Because of its thickness, cutting cardstock almost feels like carving sometimes, and the fibers can be quite maleable and forgiving. And with the bathymetric and topographic subjects of my work, I do feel, at times, that I am excavating a landscape or diving into the depths of cool, clear waters. Every piece becomes a little adventure, and with my trusty and tiny sword in hand, I enjoy conquering the world around me.

Marnie B. Karger

Marnie is the creative force behind Crafterall, a shop featuring meticulously cut and layered paper art. Her work, specializing in topographic and bathymetric map re-creation, has been featured on numerous craft, style, and design blogs, is sold at the Museum of Modern Art stores in New York and Tokyo, and is still made by hand in the basement studio of her home in Minnesota. Marnie's work was published in the collection *1,000 Handmade Greetings: Creative Cards and Clever Correspondence* (Laura McFadden, Quarry Books, 2008).

Website: crafterall.com

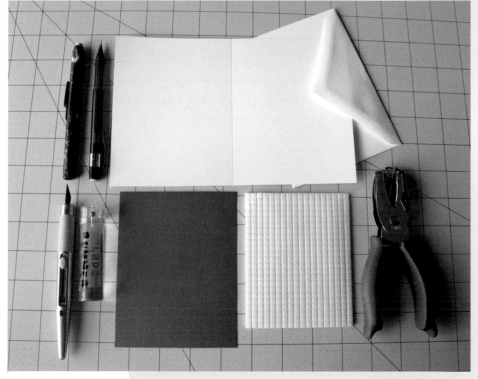

SUPPLIES AND TOOLS

White cardstock 8½ x 5½ inches
(22 x 14 cm)

Colored paper or cardstock 5¼ x 4
inches (13 x 10 cm)

Adhesive foam squares or dots ½-inch
(13 mm) diameter

Envelope or frame matted for a
5¼ x 4-inch (13 x 10 cm) piece

Straight blade

Swivel blade I use EK Success's Blade
Runner tool, but any swivel blade or
very fine scissors will work.

Fine-tip pencil

Eraser

Cutting mat

Straight edge

Bone folder

Hole punch optional, instead of swivel
blade for smaller, flat works only

Frame with mat

HOW TO MAKE THE FRAMEABLE TREE CARD

STEP 1 Score and fold the white cardstock in half and unfold. **STEP 2** With the pencil, lightly draw a basic shape of a tree trunk with branches. Keep it simple and leave at least a 1/2-inch (13 mm) margin between the sketch and the edge of the cardstock.

Tip!
Use a bone folder to score cardstock before folding and also to sharpen the fold. This gives a professional look to a handmade card.

STEP 3 Using the swivel blade, cut 1/4-inch (6 mm) ovals as the tree leaves. Start close to the inner branches and work outward. Keep a 1/4-inch (6 mm) space between the cuts If some of the oval cut-outs stay attached to the card, use the straight blade to cut these out, or gently pull from the back of the card to tear the last little bit away. It may help to lightly draw lines to give a margin for the outer leaves. **STEP 4** Continue cutting the leaves until a fully shaped tree is formed.

STEP 5 Using the straight blade and working from the tip of each branch, begin cutting the branches of the tree. Cut the branches in a narrow v-shape toward the trunk. Once all of the branches lead to the trunk, cut the trunk itself.

STEP 6 At the bottom of the trunk, cut 2-3 curves with the straight blade to resemble exposed roots.

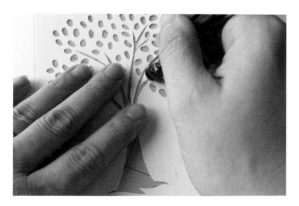

STEP 7 Carefully and slowly erase any pencil lines that show. Place one hand flat on the card to keep it steady as the other hand erases.

STEP 8 Turn the card over and attach adhesive foam squares to the back of the card, close to but not on the edges of the inner points and immediate boundary of the tree shape. This will prevent the adhesive from being seen on the front of the card. It may be necessary to cut some of the foam squares in half to fit them in a small area.

STEP 9 Peel the backing from the top of the foam squares and set the card aside.

STEP 10 Attach adhesive foam squares to the front of the colored piece of cardstock or paper, just on the corners and in the middle of each long side. Peel the backing off these squares too, so that all adhesive is showing.

STEP 11 Carefully turn over the colored cardstock and center it on the back side of the cut out portion of the card. There will be about a 1/8-inch (3 mm) margin all around.

STEP 12 Press gently to stick both pieces of cardstock together, flip the card over, fold it in half once more, and the card is done!

Variations

This tutorial can certainly be used for any size piece. If it will be framed, skip the steps that involve folding and just work with a single flat piece. Plan to frame the piece using a thick mat that will allow the foam to expand and show off the depth of the two layers for greater light and shadow play.

If working with a small piece, such as an artist trading card, use a small hole punch to make the leaves instead of a swivel blade. In keeping with the directions above, work from the inner branches of the tree, moving outward to create the canopy of leaves.

Try creating a seasonal theme by using a variety of colors and slight changes to these directions. Make a tree for each of the four seasons: For spring, cut smaller holes for buds and back with a light green or brown cardstock, or draw the buds onto the branches with an archival pen. For summer, create a full tree with dark green leaves, and for autumn create orange or red leaves with a pile of fallen leaves at the base of the tree. Winter could be bare branches layered over white.

Instead of using cardstock or paper behind the tree, try something translucent like vellum or parchment paper, then mount the piece in a floating/backless frame in front of a window or light source to let the light show through the cuts.

PERFECT JOURNEY JOURNAL

by Debra Charlesworth

I love to travel and record memories from my trips. After buying journals that didn't quite meet my needs, I decided to make my own. This journal is an exploration into mixed media techniques, and is the type of book I would use after my trip to contain photos and journaling. These books are welcomed as gifts whether they're blank and full of possibilities or filled with memories from a special trip with a friend.

SUPPLIES

Wood pieces 2 (5¹/₁₆ x 6¹/₁₆ x ⅛ inches) (13 cm x 15 cm x 3 mm)
Map mine is a library discard
Tissue paper white
Waterproof stamping ink
Matte gel medium soft/fluid and regular*
Glossy gel medium soft/fluid*
Grosgrain ribbon ¼ inch (6 mm) wide, approximately 1 yard (1 meter) long
Cardstock assorted colors
PVA bookbinding glue
Linen thread
Beeswax if the linen thread isn't waxed
Fixative (not pictured)
*Gel mediums come in a variety of thicknesses and each manufacturer has different names for them. Soft or fluid mediums are pourable with a honey-like consistency. Regular mediums are thicker and have the consistency of toothpaste.

Debra Charlesworth

Debra is a paper artist inspired by the natural surroundings of her home in Michigan's Upper Peninsula. She blogs about her crafting experiences at *Lift Bridge Cards and Crafts* and has exhibited her work at several juried art fairs. Debra has also displayed her work at the Great Lakes Showcase, a regional juried arts and crafts exhibition. In 2011, her book, *Fossils*, placed third in the 3D division.

Website: liftbridge.blogspot.com

" Why Paper?

My earliest memories of paper crafting include creating confetti to show my father, and making long paper chains for our Christmas celebrations. Although I have dabbled in many different art forms, I always return to paper. I love how this common material can be transformed into books, boxes, cards, and more. I am particularly drawn to how things are constructed, probably because my formal education is in engineering. My art work is very practical, and generally begins with a need or problem that is solved by making an object with paper. "

TOOLS

Brush
Bone folder
Corner rounder (not pictured)
Tapestry sewing needle blunt end
Cutting mat
Scissors
Craft knife
Paper trimmer
Rubber stamps images used here are by
   Club Stamp
Cork board or foam mat (not pictured)
File or sandpaper
Awl or paper piercer
Ruler
Ink blending tool or sponge

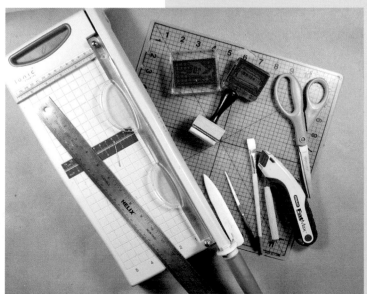

HOW TO MAKE THE JOURNAL COVERS

STEP 1 Roughly cut a piece of map paper so that it is slightly larger than the wood pieces that will become the covers of the book.

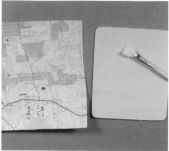

STEP 2 Paint a generous amount of regular gel medium on one side of a wood piece.

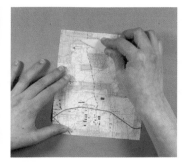

STEP 3 Place the map paper on top of the gel medium and burnish gently with a bone folder to eliminate any air bubbles. Since the paper is wet, burnishing roughly may tear the paper.

STEP 4 Let the gel medium partially dry for approximately two minutes. Tear edges of the paper and rip to expose part of the wood surface beneath.

STEP 5 Let the gel medium dry completely. **STEP 6** Trim the excess map paper with a craft knife.

STEP 7 Use inks with ink blending tool to cover the surface as desired. The ink will absorb differently into the torn and whole parts of the paper, creating an aged look.

STEP 8 Stamp the images on scratch paper and trim around each image using scissors to create a mask.

STEP 9 Tear a piece of tissue paper approximately 2-3 inches (5-7.6 cm) wide, and longer than the height of the cover.
STEP 10 Use waterproof ink and a variety of rubber stamps to stamp on the tissue paper. Be sure to stamp off the torn edge to create a more natural background.

STEP 11a To keep an image in the foreground, cover it with the mask created in step 8 and stamp over it with the desired image.

STEP 11b This is how it should look after two images are stamped. Continue stamping until the tissue paper is covered as desired with images.

STEP 12 Apply fluid glossy gel medium to the left hand side of the cover. Note that any water based inks will run slightly. Carefully lay the tissue paper on top of the gel medium. Gently pat the paper into the medium, taking care not to rip the tissue paper. Wrinkles add to the character of the design.

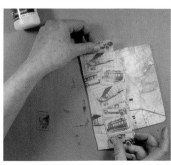

STEP 13 Repeat steps 2-12 on the back cover, taking care to apply the fluid gloss medium on the right hand side of the cover to create a mirror image.

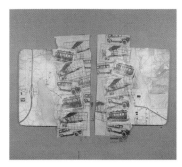

STEP 14 Let the gel medium dry thoroughly, then trim the excess tissue paper on each cover with a craft knife or scissors.

STEP 15 Coat the tissue paper on both covers with fluid glossy gel medium to seal the tissue paper onto the cover. Gloss medium will make the tissue paper transparent, so that the map underneath will be seen.

STEP 16 (photo above) After both covers have thoroughly dried, use a file or sandpaper to sand the edges.
STEP 17 (photo above right) Use an ink blending tool to apply brown ink to the edges of the cover. Spray a coat of fixative on the cover to prevent water-based inks from running. Let it dry.

STEP 18 Coat the entire cover with a thin layer of fluid matte gel medium. This will give the covers an even satin sheen. If desired, mix matte and glossy gel mediums to create a shinier finish.

HOW TO MAKE THE INSIDE PAGES

STEP 1 Prepare the inside pages: Trim cardstock to 9⁷/₈ x 5¹/₂ inches (25 x 14 cm). Cut the paper so that the grain runs vertically, and the paper folds easily in half. To determine paper grain, refer to Tips! box on page 57.

STEP 2 Fold each paper in half, sharpening the fold with a bone folder. Each of these pieces is called a signature.

STEP 3 Pierce holes along the fold of the paper at 1, 1¹/₂, 1⁷/₈, 3⁷/₈, 4¹/₄, and 4³/₄ inches (2.5 cm, 3.8 cm, 4.8 cm, 9.8 cm, 10.8 cm, and 12.1 cm) from the left edge. If a different width of ribbon is used, make sure the spacing between the 2nd and 3rd holes and 4th and 5th holes will accommodate the chosen ribbon.

STEP 4 Pierce the remaining signatures with the awl using the first piece as a template. Keep the signatures oriented in the same direction for the rest of the project.

HOW TO SEW THE BOOK BLOCK

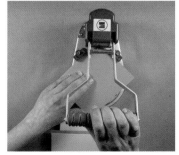

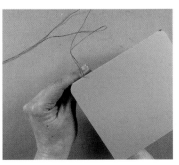

This is how it should look when you are done with your piercings.

STEP 5 Use a corner rounder to round the corners of each folded page. Make sure to use a corner rounder that can punch through two layers of cardstock.

STEP 1 Cut a piece of linen thread 55 inches (140 cm) long. If a different number or size of signature is used, cut a length of linen thread equal to the number of signatures multiplied by the height of each signature.
STEP 2 If the thread is unwaxed, run it through a block of beeswax several times to coat the thread.

STEP 3 Thread the needle with the waxed linen thread. Hold one signature so the thumb is inside the fold, and the remaining fingers are outside. Enter the left most hole and pull the thread inside, leaving a 3-inch (7.6 cm) tail outside the signature.

STEP 4 Pull the thread up through the second hole, pulling the thread taut.

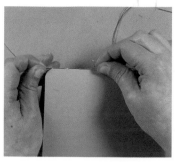

STEP 5 When pulling the thread taut, pull along the length of the thread, never perpendicular to the stitching.

STEP 6 Lay a 3-inch (7.6 cm) length of grosgrain ribbon between the second and third holes. Put the needle in the third hole and pull the thread back into the signature. Pull the thread taut, making sure to trap the ribbon between the folded signature and the linen thread.

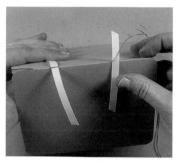

STEP 7 Pull the needle up through the fourth hole, and lay a second piece of grosgrain ribbon between the 4th and 5th holes. Pull the needle through the 5th hole into the signature, trapping the ribbon between the paper and the thread. Pull the needle out of the signature through the 6th hole.

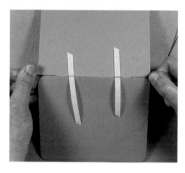

STEP 8 Check that the thread is taut along the entire signature.

STEP 9 Pick up a second signature, and place on top of the first signature. Place the thumb inside the second signature and hold both signatures with the hand on the outside.

STEP 10 Stitch down the signature, entering at the 6th hole, out the 5th hole, and so on until exiting the signature through the 1st hole.

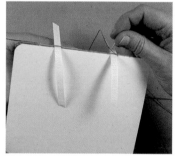

STEP 10a Make sure that the thread is taut.

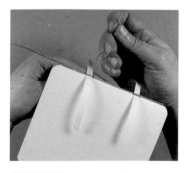

STEP 10b Trap each ribbon between the thread and signature.

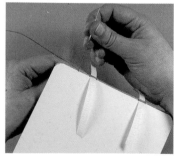

STEP 10c Continue to stitch until the signature end is reached.

STEP 11 Once completed it should look like this.

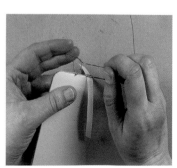

STEP 12 Tie a knot with the tail from step 4.

 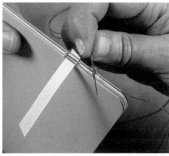 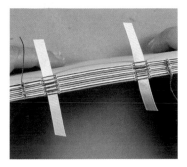

STEP 13 Pick up a third signature, and sew back to the 6th hole. Put the needle between the stitch from the 6th hole in the 1st signature to the 6th hole in the 2nd signature. Pull the thread to form a small loop, and drop the needle in the loop. This stitch is known as a kettle stitch and serves to tie each new signature to the previous signature.

STEP 14 Add the remaining signatures by sewing along the length of each and using a kettle stitch at the ends to form the book block.

STEP 15 After the last signature, form the last kettle stitch, and then cut the thread approximately 2 inches (5 cm) from the stitch. Trim the ribbon and linen thread so that the tails are approximately 2 inches (5 cm) long.

HOW TO ASSEMBLE THE BOOK

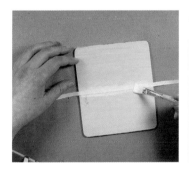 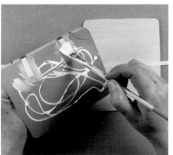  

STEP 1 On the back of each book cover, mark "spine" in pencil along the edge with the tissue paper.
STEP 2 Cut a piece of grosgrain ribbon approximately 30 inches (76 cm) long. Place the center of the ribbon perpendicular to the spine edge of a book cover and glue in place.

STEP 3 Apply bookbinding glue to the entire surface of one of the outside pages of the book block. Hold the book block so that the page with glue isn't touching the other pages of the book.

STEP 4 Spread the glue to the edge of the page. The glue should be thin and evenly spread.

STEP 5 Place the book block on one of the covers of the book, making sure that the spine is on the correct edge of the cover.

STEP 6 Burnish the page onto the wooden cover and let dry until the glue is set (approximately 30 minutes). If desired, wrap cover in waxed paper and place the entire book under a weight to add uniform pressure to the drying surface.

STEP 7 Wrap the ribbon around the book block and glue into place.

STEP 8 Apply glue to the remaining outside cover of the book, and place onto the second wooden piece, carefully centering it on the cover, and burnishing the paper onto the board.

STEP 9 Use a slightly damp piece of paper towel to wipe up any excess glue. Dry under a weight as in step 6. If desired, add a stamped quote or image to the cover.

FRAMEABLE GIFT CARD

by Dawn M. Cardona

Sometimes the best part about receiving a present is the sweet message hidden within the attached gift card. Make a statement with your next gift by not only sending your message of love, but also giving the recipient a daily reminder of your affection with this frameable gift card. Few things communicate feelings more than a simple, yet beautiful, flower!

Dawn M. Cardona

Dawn is a self-taught artist with an obsession for paper scraps and vintage ephemera. She likes to garden, jump in rain puddles, and drink vanilla lattes with her husband.

Blog: cutpaperpaste.com

Why Paper?

I love working with paper for many reasons, but what I appreciate most about this medium is that it is readily available. It's everywhere and comes in all colors, shapes, and sizes. I never have trouble finding inspiration when working with paper. In my experience, I have been able to build up my collection through trading my art with others in exchange for paper from all over the world. It's fascinating to me that a piece of paper can travel through time and space, completely unscathed. In a way, it is a magical thing and somehow that magic comes to life when it is turned into a work of art.

SUPPLIES AND TOOLS

Cutting mat
Paper cutter
Rotary cutter pinking and perforating blades
Craft knife
Heavy textured cardstock pink, white, 1 sheet
 of each
Scrap paper 6 different patterns and solid colors
Bone folder
Circle punch 1 inch (2.5 cm)
Hole punch 1/4 inch (6 mm)
Patterned Japanese washi tape
Message stamp
Ink pad
Quilling paper light green, dark green,
 1/8 inch (3 mm)
Quilling tool slotted
Craft glue
Pencil
Scissors
Steel ruler
Yarn or string/ribbon
Gift box
Tweezers optional

Tip!
This gift card works best with gifts given in boxes. Since boxes come in all sizes, adjust the measurements so the card doesn't extend beyond the edges of the box.

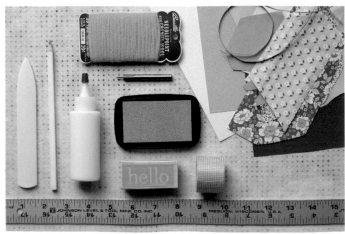

HOW TO MAKE THE CARD FRAME AND CANVAS

STEP 1 Create the frame: Cut a piece of white cardstock that measures 3³/₄ x 6¹/₄ inches (9.5 x 16 cm). This piece will serve as a frame for the portion of the gift card that is removable.

STEP 2 With the textured side facing down, place the cardstock on a cutting mat and measure in ⁵/₈ inch (16 mm) from the left and right edges of the 6¹/₄-inch (16 cm) measurement. Score each edge using a bone folder, but don't fold in the edges just yet.

STEP 3 Insert the pinking blade into the rotary cutter. Use it and a steel ruler to trim ¹/₈ inch (3 mm) off the left and right edges, giving the cardstock a decorative edge.

STEP 4 Fold in the scored edges. When folded, it will measure 5 inches (13 cm) across.

STEP 5a To create a message, ink the stamp thoroughly and center it over the folded white frame and press. Set aside to allow the ink to dry.

STEP 5b Perhaps include a handwritten message on the card.

STEP 6 Create the removable canvas: Cut a piece of pink cardstock that measures 3⁵/₈ x 4⁷/₈ inches (9 x 12 cm).

STEP 7 With the textured side facing down and the cardstock lengthwise on a cutting mat, measure in ⁵/₈ inch (16 mm) from the left and right edges, and lightly draw lines using a ruler and pencil.

STEP 8 Insert the perforating blade into the rotary cutter. Use it and a steel ruler to perforate the pink cardstock along the penciled lines. Set aside.

HOW TO MAKE THE FLOWER

STEP 1 Make the flower: Punch six circles with the 1-inch (2.5 cm) circle punch. Each circle should be punched from a different pattern or color of scrap paper.

STEP 2 Fold each circle in half with the patterned or colored side facing up.

STEP 3 Apply glue to the back of a folded circle half and smooth it evenly with a finger. Adhere the half to another circle half.

STEP 4 Repeat until all of the circles have been glued together. DO NOT glue the first circle to the last circle that was attached. Compress the flower and set it under a book to prevent the petals from warping while the glue dries.

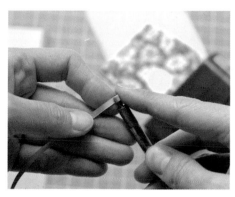

STEP 5a Make the leaves: Insert a 6-inch (15 cm) strip of light green quilling paper into the quilling tool slot and roll until reaching the strip end.

STEP 5b The end can be torn if the strip seems too long.

STEP 6 Allow the coil to relax and slip it off the tool. Pinch it to form a leaf (teardrop) shape.

STEP 7 Apply a tiny amount of glue to the end of the strip, hold in place for a moment, and trim excess paper. Repeat with a 7.5-inch (19 cm) strip to make the second leaf.

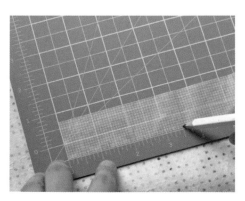

STEP 8a Adhere the washi tape to the cutting mat, make a pencil mark at 3½ inches (9 cm), and cut the tape

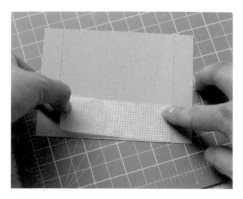

STEP 8b Center the tape along the bottom edge of the pink cardstock and adhere it. Smooth out any air bubbles.

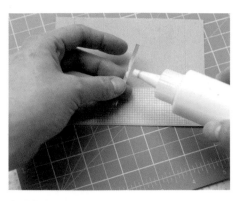

STEP 9a Cut a 2½-inch (5.5 cm) strip of dark green quilling paper as the flower stem. Snip a V-notch at the bottom of the stem. Smooth a thin layer of glue on the back of the strip.

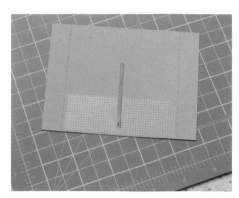

STEP 9b Center and glue the stem on the pink cardstock overlapping the washi tape.

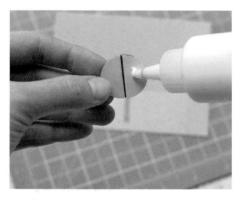

STEP 10a Apply a thin, even layer of glue to the back of the flower.

STEP 10b Glue the flower at the top of the stem, slightly overlapping it.

STEP 11 Apply a thin, even layer of glue to the back of the small leaf and position it on the right side of the stem with its tip pointing outward. Tweezers may be helpful. Glue the larger leaf on the left side of the stem, lower than the small leaf. Each leaf should slightly overlap the stem.

HOW TO ASSEMBLE THE GIFT CARD

STEP 1 Spread glue on the back of the pink cardstock–ends only!–taking care to not extend the glue past the perforations.

STEP 2 With the folded flaps of the white cardstock opened and facing up, center the pink cardstock over the message and glue in place.

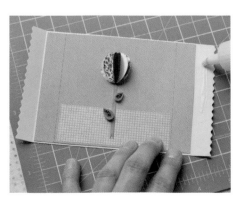

STEP 3 Apply glue to the back of the white cardstock flaps and fold them over the pink cardstock. Press firmly to ensure there are no air pockets. Allow to dry.

STEP 4 Use the cutting mat measurements as a guide to mark ³/₄ inch (19 mm) from the top and bottom, and ¹/₄ inch (6 mm) in from the left and right edges of the white cardstock.

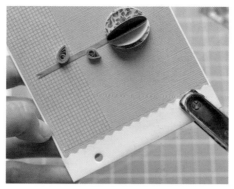

STEP 5 Center and punch a hole over each pencil mark.

STEP 6 Measure and cut the yarn, string, or ribbon to accommodate the gift box dimensions.

STEP 7 Insert one end of the yarn up through the bottom of one of the holes and down through the top of the adjacent hole.

STEP 8 Pull yarn through the holes so there is enough to wrap across the back of the box and up through a hole on the opposite side of the gift tag.

STEP 9 Insert the yarn down through the top of the last hole, bringing it around to the back of the box. Tie the loose ends in a bow and the gift is finished!

Tips!
Be sure to share with the recipient that the hidden message can be revealed by carefully tearing along the perforated edges of the pink cardstock.

Once removed, the flower artwork can be framed and enjoyed!

WEDDING CAKE CARD

by Agnieszka Malyszek

Weddings are such special occasions, I like to give a handmade card to mark the day. This elegant design features fringed flowers that are arranged to resemble a layered wedding cake. The embossed background paper and rhinestones add a bit of glitz and glamour.

SUPPLIES AND TOOLS

Cardstock gray, 1 sheet
Cardstock white, yellow, textured, 1 sheet of each
  (Bazzill Basic Paper)
Rubber stamp Antique Flower Background (Hero Arts)
Clear embossing ink pad
Embossing powder white
Quilling paper pale yellow, ¼ inch (6 mm)
Quilling tool
Metal ruler
Craft knife
Pencil
Detail scissors
Glue fine-tip applicator or apply with a needle
Tape runner or double-stick tape
Bent tip tweezers
Embossing heat tool
Container
Spoon
Adhesive foam squares
Mini binder clip
Rhinestones 5 mm, self-adhesive, 18 (Kaisercraft)
Computer printer
Bone folder to score cardstock optional

Agnieszka Malyszek

Agnieszka was born in Poland and currently lives in the U.K. As a graduate of Maritime Academy, she works for an IT company that operates in the shipping market. Paper crafting is her relaxing hobby. Agnieszka started with origami and quilling, and soon became an avid card maker. She has been published in *Paper Crafts Magazine* and *CARDS* magazine.

Blog: justmadefrompaper.blogspot.com

" Why Paper?

I love being creative in all forms. I started my paper crafting adventure in 2009 by making cards for my friends and family, and I've been completely addicted to this hobby ever since. My favorite aspect of paper crafting is creating unique, original items with a personal touch. "

HOW TO MAKE THE WEDDING CAKE CARD

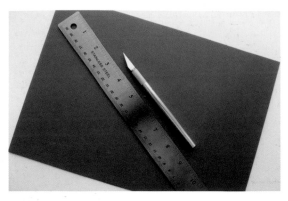

STEP 1 Cut, score, and fold a 5³/₄ x 8-inch (14.6 x 20.3 cm) piece of gray cardstock to make a rectangular card that measures 5³/₄ x 4 inches (14.6 x 10.1 cm).

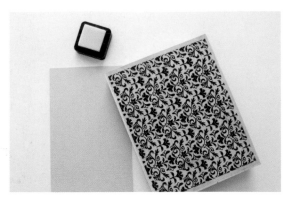

STEP 2 Cut a 6¹/₄ x 3¹/₂-inch (15.9 x 8.9 cm) textured yellow cardstock rectangle. Use clear embossing ink to stamp the background image. Allow an inch (25 mm) of open space at one end of the cardstock so it can be held easily while heat embossing the stamped image. Trim excess after the embossing is finished.

STEP 3 Sprinkle white embossing powder over the stamped image with the aid of a spoon. Hold the cardstock over a container and gently tap the back to eliminate any excess powder.

STEP 4 Use the embossing heat tool to heat the powder until it melts. Do not overheat the image as this causes the powder to scorch and the cardstock to curl.

STEP 5 Cut a 5¹/₂ x 3³/₄-inch (14 x 9.5 cm) rectangle of white textured cardstock.

STEP 6 Adhere the white rectangle to the center of the gray card with a tape runner or double-sided tape. Adhere the embossed rectangle to the white layer in the same manner.

STEP 7 Fringe an 8-inch (20 cm) strip of pale yellow quilling paper to make each flower. (make 21)

STEP 8 Use a quilling tool to roll each strip into a tight coil, apply a small amount of glue to the end, press in place, slip coil off tool, and allow the glue to dry for a few minutes. Gently fluff out the fringe with fingertips.

Tips!

Stack up to three quilling strips at a time and use detail scissors to fringe the paper crosswise repeatedly, working slowly and carefully to ensure even cuts.

The use of a mini binder clip allows cuts of equal depth to be made quite easily, and best of all, helps to avoid cutting across the strip completely.

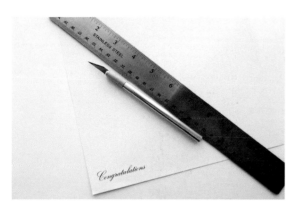

STEP 9 Print out the word Congratulations (Kunstler script, 35 pt) in black on a sheet of textured white cardstock. Cut a 2⅓ x 3½-inch (6 x 9 cm) rectangle with the word centered about ½ inch (13 mm) from the lower edge.

STEP 10 Referring to the photo of the finished card, use a pencil and ruler to draw light lines as placement guides for the rhinestones and fringed flowers. Start by sticking on the bottom row of rhinestones and work upward. Apply a small amount of glue to the bottom of each fringed flower and place them with tweezers.

STEP 11 Use adhesive foam squares to attach the small white rectangle to the center of the card.

STEP 12 Give or send to the lucky couple with your very best wishes for a lifetime of happiness!

FRINGED FLOWER CARD

by Agnieszka Malyszek

Paper fringing is one of those things that card makers either enjoy or detest! I happen to find it relaxing and fun to do, and enjoy the beautiful end result. The cheerful design of this card is suitable for so many occasions, and it can serve a dual purpose when placed atop a gift instead of a traditional bow. Perhaps the recipient will choose to give it an even longer life by preserving the card in a shadow box-style frame.

SUPPLIES AND TOOLS

Cardstock white, textured, 1 sheet
(Bazzill Basic Paper)
Cardstock lilac, textured, 1 sheet
(Metallic Paper Stack by DCWV)
Copy paper pink, fuchsia, 1 sheet of each
Quilling paper cream, 1/4 x 16 inches
(6 mm x 40 cm)
Metal ruler
Craft knife
Pencil
Detail scissors
Fringe scissors
Glue fine-tip applicator or apply with a
needle
Double-sided tape or tape runner
Adhesive foam squares
Mini binder clip
Bone folder for scoring cardstock
(optional)

HOW TO MAKE THE FLOWER CARD

STEP 1 Cut, score, and fold an 8¹/₂ x 4¹/₄-inch (22 x 11 cm) piece of textured white cardstock to make a square, top-fold card that measures 4¹/₄ x 4¹/₄ inches (11 x 11 cm).

STEP 2 Cut a 4 x 4-inch (10 x 10 cm) square of textured lilac cardstock. Cut and remove a 2¹/₄ x 2¹/₄-inch (6 x 6 cm) inner square. Use a tape runner or double-sided tape to adhere the smaller square to the center of the white card.

STEP 3a Apply adhesive foam squares to the back of the larger square.

STEP 3b Firmly press the square onto the center of the card, creating a recessed effect.

STEP 4 Create the finely fringed flower center: Stack three 16-inch (40 cm) strips of cream quilling paper and use detail scissors to fringe the paper crosswise repeatedly, working slowly and carefully to make even cuts. The use of a mini binder clip allows cuts of equal depth to be made quite easily, and best of all, helps to avoid cutting across the strip completely.

STEP 5 Tear the ends of the three fringed strips and join them end to end with a small amount of glue. Roll this long fringed strip into a tight coil, apply a small amount of glue to the end, press in place, and allow the glue to dry.

STEP 6 Cut a $\frac{5}{8}$ x 11-inch (1.5 x 28 cm) strip of pink paper. Make fine, even cuts with detail scissors across the width of the strip.

STEP 7 Apply a small amount of glue to one end of the fringed pink strip and roll it firmly and evenly around the cream center. Glue the end.

STEP 8 Use fringe scissors to cut two strips of fuchsia paper, each measuring 1¼ x 11 inches (3 x 28 cm). Join the strips end to end as in Step 5.

STEP 9 Apply a small amount of glue to the end of the fringed fuchsia strip and adhere it to the flower center, joining where the pink strip ended. Roll the fuchsia strip firmly and evenly around the pink center. Glue the end.

STEP 10 Open the flower by gently pressing the petals outward. Then curl them downward using a scissors blade as if curling paper ribbon.

STEP 11 Use detail scissors to taper the fuchsia petal tips for a natural look.

STEP 12 Apply glue to the back of the flower center and adhere the flower to the center of the card. Give or send to someone very special!

Agnieszka Malyszek
Wedding Cake Card
(page 100)
Fringed Flower Card
(page 104)
Blog: **justmadefrom
paper.blogspot.com**

Ann Martin
Teardrop Orb Pendant
(page 59)
Antique Key Pendant
(page 65)
Makigami Pendant Flower
(page 78)
Website: **allthingspaper.net**

Casey Starks
Citrus Slice Coasters
(page 24)
Blog: **vitaminihandmade.
blogspot.com**
Shops: **vitamini.etsy.com**
and **vitamodern.etsy.com**

Danielle Connel
Tiger Lily Fascinator
(page 46)
Shop: **shinymonkey
buttons.etsy.com**

Debra Charlesworth
Perfect Journey Journal
(page 88)
Website: **liftbridge.
blogspot.com**

Allison Patrick
Phone Book Letter Holder
(page 12)
Website: **zipper
8lighting.com**
Blog: **the3rsblog.word
press.com**

Benjamin John Coleman
Loosely Braided Makigami
Pendant (page 72)
Websites: **origamibonsai.
org** and **benagami.com**

Cecelia Louie
Mysterious Stationery Box
(page 32)
Blog: **craftingcreatures.
blogspot.com**

Dawn M. Cardona
Frameable Gift Card
(page 94)
Blog: **cutpaperpaste.com**

Jenny Jafek-Jones
Crepe Paper Lilacs
(page 16)
Website: **thecrimson
poppy.com**
Blog: **thecrimson
poppy.tumblr.com**

Kristen Magee
Candle Luminaries (page 9)
Websites: **papercrave.com**
and **domestifluff.com**

Linda Thalmann
Fine Paper Yarn Necklace
(page 68)
Website: **paperphine.com**

Marnie B. Karger
Frameable Tree Card
(page 84)
Website: **crafterall.com**

Richela Fabian Morgan
Everyday Tote Bag
(page 51)
Website: **richelafabian**
morgan.com

Licia Politis
Jungle Beads Necklace
(page 56)

Lorraine Nam
Silhouette Portrait Art
(page 41)
Website: **lorrainenam.com**

Patricia Zapata
Tiered Garland Ornament
(page 22)
Website: **alittlehut.com**

Stefani Tadio
Sticky Notes Notepad
Holder (page 28)
Website: **pinetree**
designs.com

TEMPLATES

All templates are actual sizes. Because there is printing on both
sides of pages 108-111, you may wish to photocopy the templates.

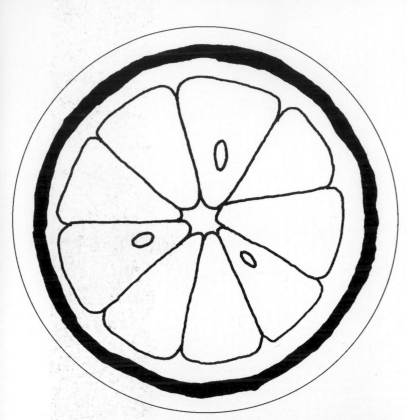

Citrus Slice Coasters
page 24-27

Tiger Lily Fascinator
page 46-49

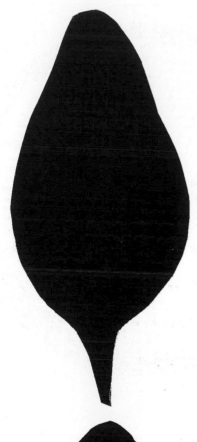

Crepe Paper Lilacs
page 16-21

Tiered Garland Ornament
page 22-23

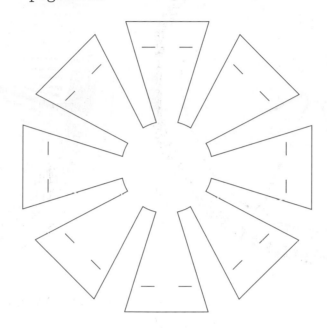

Sticky Notes Notepad Holder
page 28-31

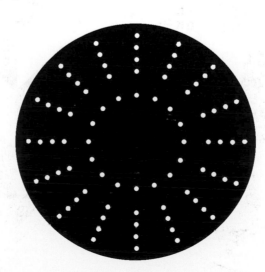

Oval Template

Flower Template A

Flower Template B

Published by Tuttle Publishing, an imprint of Periplus Editions (HK) Ltd.

www.tuttlepublishing.com

Library of Congress Cataloging-in-Publication data in progess

ISBN 978-0-8048-4366-9

Distributed by

North America, Latin America & Europe
Tuttle Publishing
364 Innovation Drive
North Clarendon, VT
05759-9436 U.S.A.
Tel: 1 (802) 773-8930
Fax: 1 (802) 773-6993
info@tuttlepublishing.com
www.tuttlepublishing.com

Asia Pacific
Berkeley Books Pte. Ltd.
61 Tai Seng Avenue #02-12
Singapore 534167
Tel: (65) 6280-1330
Fax: (65) 6280-6290
inquiries@periplus.com.sg
www.periplus.com

16 15 14 13
10 9 8 7 6 5 4 3 2 1

Printed in Singapore
1303 CP

TUTTLE PUBLISHING is a registered trademark of Tuttle Publishing, a division of Periplus Editions (HK) Ltd.

THE TUTTLE STORY "BOOKS TO SPAN THE EAST AND WEST"

Most people are surprised to learn that the world's largest publisher of books on Asia had its humble beginnings in the tiny American state of Vermont. The company's founder, Charles Tuttle, came from a New England family steeped in publishing, and his first love was books—especially old and rare editions.

Tuttle's father was a noted antiquarian dealer in Rutland, Vermont. Young Charles honed his knowledge of the trade working in the family bookstore, and later in the rare books section of Columbia University Library. His passion for beautiful books—old and new—never wavered thoughout his long career as a bookseller and publisher.

After graduating from Harvard, Tuttle enlisted in the military and in 1945 was sent to Tokyo to work on General Douglas MacArthur's staff. He was tasked with helping to revive the Japanese publishing industry, which had been utterly devastated by the war. When his tour of duty was completed, he left the military, married a talented and beautiful singer, Reiko Chiba, and in 1948 began several successful business ventures.

To his astonishment, Tuttle discovered that postwar Tokyo was actually a book-lover's paradise. He befriended dealers in the Kanda district and began supplying rare Japanese editions to American libraries. He also imported American books to sell to the thousands of GIs stationed in Japan. By 1949, Tuttle's business was thriving, and he opened Tokyo's very first English-language bookstore in the Takashimaya Department Store in Ginza, to great success. Two years later, he began publishing books to fulfill the growing interest of foreigners in all things Asian.

Though a westerner, Tuttle was hugely instrumental in bringing a knowledge of Japan and Asia to a world hungry for information about the East. By the time of his death in 1993, he had published over 6,000 books on Asian culture, history and art—a legacy honored by Emperor Hirohito in 1983 with the "Order of the Sacred Treasure," the highest honor Japan bestows upon non-Japanese.

The Tuttle company today maintains an active backlist of some 1,500 titles, many of which have been continuously in print since the 1950s and 1960s—a great testament to Charles Tuttle's skill as a publisher. More than 60 years after its founding, Tuttle Publishing is more active today than at any time in its history, still inspired by Charles Tuttle's core mission—to publish fine books to span the East and West and provide a greater understanding of each.